Never Bow to Racism

Never Bow to Racism

A Personal Account

of the Ecumenical Struggle

Baldwin Sjollema

**World Council
of Churches**
Publications

NEVER BOW TO RACISM
A Personal Account of the Ecumenical Struggle

WCC Publications is the book publishing programme of the World Council of Churches. Founded in 1948, the WCC promotes Christian unity in faith, witness and service for a just and peaceful world. A global fellowship, the WCC brings together more than 345 Protestant, Orthodox, Anglican and other churches representing more than 550 million Christians in 110 countries and works cooperatively with the Roman Catholic Church.

Opinions expressed in WCC Publications are those of the authors.

Scripture quotations are from the New Revised Standard Version Bible, © copyright 1989 by the Division of Christian Education of the National Council of the Churches of Christ in the USA. Used by permission.

Cover and book design: Michelle Cook / 4 Seasons Book Design
Cover image: Peter Magubane, photo of angry crowd mourning at the funeral of Hector Petersen, the first victim of the 1976 Soweto youth uprising.

ISBN: 978-2-8254-1654-9

World Council of Churches
150 route de Ferney, P.O. Box 2100
1211 Geneva 2, Switzerland
http://publications.oikoumene.org

CONTENTS

For my wife, Jet,
and for our children,
Suzanne†, Inge, Anne-Marie, Emilie, and Frederik
and our grandchildren,
Fanny, Clément, Mathilde, Loic, Alexis, Max, Zoé, Ella and Augustin

Preface

I do not write to hold on, but to let go, to set
memory free, to let myself be: myself and
all those who allowed me to be what I am now –
whatever that may be!
– Chris Minnaar, *The Changing Face
of African Literature*

Those who cannot remember the past are
condemned to repeat it.
– George Santayana, *The Life of Reason*, 1905

We live in history, and we also live with its consequences. We are not only the objects of history, but also its subjects. We cannot stand aside from it. We also make history, and we make decisions that affect our lives and those of others. We make deliberate choices and ask ourselves whether we are right.

During the 20th century, we were subjected to the traumatic experience of war and annihilation. We were confronted with violence and destruction as well as prosperity and happiness on a scale as never before. It was indeed, as Eric Hobsbawm has written, an age of extremes.

The 20th century was also the time of the ecumenical movement, and the creation of the World Council of Churches (WCC) as its most visible and outspoken instrument.

From its very beginning, the WCC was confronted with some of the world's most crucial socio-economic and political issues. One of those was racism, which dangerously threatened the unity of humankind.

Today, we have to admit that, in spite of all our efforts, we have unfortunately not made much headway in combating racism. As the many crises in our world continue and intensify, it is important to take stock of what has been done.

The welfare state was one of the social victories of the 20th century. By now, we have forgotten the political and social traumas of mass insecurity: we have forgotten why we inherited those welfare states and what brought them about. The young generation takes social stability for granted and demands less state interference and less taxation. We describe our goals exclusively in economic terms: growth, prosperity, efficiency, output, interest rates, stock markets. But these cannot be ends in themselves.

My question is whether, in our 21st century, we are as committed to ideals as we were in the 20th. The 20th century was the time of the ecumenical ideal, but is that ideal still as alive as it was then? Do we remember why the ecumenical ideal came into being? Why was the WCC created and what was and is it all about? How many churches and Christians have become introverted and interested only in their own small worlds, just as politicians have become nationalistic.

The general feeling tends to be: that was then, and this is now. All we have to learn is not to repeat the past. We seek to forget rather than to remember; to deny continuity and proclaim novelty on every possible occasion. The 20th century is hardly behind us, but already its fears and ideals are slipping into obscurity. Lessons are ignored. Perhaps this is not surprising: the recent past is hardest to know and understand. But one of the most dangerous illusions today is that we live in a time without precedent, that what is happening now is new, that the past has nothing to teach us.

Whether we like it or not, the past hangs heavily over the present. We cannot escape history. The message today that the past is behind us and we may now advance without the burden of past errors into a different and better world is no doubt in part due to globalization. But we should not forget that the economic globalization of the 19th century was no less disruptive; simply, its implications were felt by fewer people.

This lack of concern about memories of the past is worrying. We seem to have lost the understanding of what war means. And countries that won the war seem to have lost peace. Sometimes the holocaust, the genocide of the Jews, is presented as an exceptional crime, the 20th-century evil never equalled before or since. But are we that sure it cannot be repeated elsewhere? Terrible genocides have already taken place since.

One of the characteristics of the 20th century was the rise and fall of the state. After the emergence of autonomous nation-states during the early decades, we witnessed the decline of their power at the hands of multinational corporations and transnational institutions. Also, and most important with regard to issues of racism, we see the accelerated and uncontrolled movement of people within and between continents. How do we, how *can* we live together as people of different cultures, races, and religions? Unless we take these issues far more seriously, we run the risk of seeing similarly evil situations arise in the future.

When the churches met at the assembly of the WCC in Uppsala in 1968, they were confronted with a world in turmoil. One of the major issues was racism. The assembly decided that priority attention had to be given to combating white racism with particular emphasis on Southern and South Africa. We were living in the post-colonial period when the political independence of the former colonies had almost been achieved, but not their economic liberation.

The Uppsala assembly requested the WCC to develop a programme within the WCC itself that would give the example to the member churches, and this is how the Programme to Combat Racism (PCR) came into being. It was controversial from the very beginning because of the decisions that were taken, in particular with regard to the grants to liberation movements by its Special Fund to Combat Racism. And later the debate became heated because of the WCC's call for disinvestment by multinational corporations from South Africa and for an end to bank loans to the apartheid regime. Many wondered whether it was right for the churches to involve themselves in socio-economic and political questions. Should their mandate not be limited to preaching the gospel? We were criticized and attacked by some of our key member churches and by both secular and church media for being one-sided and transgressing our mandate. We were considered too progressive, playing into the hands of extremists and communists. Why was all this necessary? Was there not a more peaceful way of doing things?

I have tried to write part of the story of the WCC's Programme to Combat Racism, the part that I know. With all the mistakes that we no doubt made, I believe it is worthwhile to remember the recent past and to try and see PCR's history in the context of that ecumenical period, and as part of the history of the second half of the 20th century. What was it that was demanded from us and how did we try to respond to the challenge before us? How did the churches react to the demands made by the racially oppressed, particularly in Southern and South Africa? What was apartheid about, how did it come into being and what was needed to overcome this particular evil? Of course, I don't pretend to have all the answers. But I hope this book may be seen as a contribution to clarifying what we were after.

But there is another reason for writing. I want to give an account of what drove me personally to involve myself in this ecumenical challenge. In hindsight, I see my involvement in the work of the WCC as a direct sequence of my experience in the Second World War. The guiding element in my life has been resistance; resistance to injustice and in particular to racial injustice. That did not make life easy, either for me or for those around me. Because the PCR took the bull by the horns, it was highly controversial. The fact that we did so became the hope of many finally to see the beast of racism tamed.

Thus this book is an attempt to render an account to the next generation – and in particular to my children and grandchildren – and to describe my ecumenical and my personal experience, in the hope that it may stimulate them and perhaps others on their road as well.

Perhaps past experience can help to understand the perennial complexity of the issues of life that we continue to face today.

Acknowledgments

I want to express special gratitude to my friend and former colleague, Thomas Wieser, who greatly encouraged me while I was writing and who commented on various drafts. I owe thanks to Joan Cambitsis for her interest and patience, and her willingness to correct my manuscript and turn it into readable English.

Theo Witvliet, Ulrich Becker, Rob van Drimmelen, and Dwain Epps have considerably helped me by reading early drafts and by providing me with most helpful comments. Chuck Harper made available material on truth and reconciliation commissions in different parts of the world. To my former colleague at the International Labour Office, Bill Ratteree, I owe particular thanks for advising me on the chapter concerning the ILO.

Finally, I am most grateful to the World Council of Churches for publishing my book.

Abbreviations

AACC	All Africa Conference of Churches
ANC	African National Congress
BCC	British Council of Churches
CCIA	Commission of the Churches on International Affairs
CCME	Churches' Commission for Migrants in Europe
CCPD	Commission on the Churches' Participation in Development
CEC	Conference of European Churches
CIMADE	Comité inter-mouvement auprès des évacués : Inter-movement committee for aid to evacuees
CLSA	Christian League of Southern Africa
CWME	Commission on World Mission and Evangelism
CWS	Church World Service
DRMC	Dutch Reformed Mission Church
EABC	European-American Banking Corporation
EDCS	Ecumenical Development Cooperative Society
EIRIS	Ethical Investment Research and Information Service
EKD	Evangelische Kirche in Deutschland: Evangelical Church in Germany
ELTSA	End Loans to South Africa
EMPSA	Ecumenical Monitoring Programme in South Africa
EU	European Union
GRAE	Revolutionary Government of Angola in Exile

ICCR	Interfaith Center on Corporate Responsibility
ICEM	Intergovernmental Committee for European Migration
ICN	International Christian Network
IEC	Independent Electoral Commission
IFOR	International Fellowship of Reconciliation
ILO	International Labour Office
IMC	International Missionary Council
IUEF	International University Exchange Fund
LWF	Lutheran World Federation
MPLA	People's Movement for the Liberation of Angola
NATO	North Atlantic Treaty Organization
NGOs	Non-governmental organizations
NLM	National liberation movement
OAU	Organization of African Unity
PAC	Pan Africanist Congress of Azania
PCR	Programme to Combat Racism
PLO	Palestinian Liberation Organization
SACBC	Southern African Catholic Bishops' Conference
SACC	South African Council of Churches
SACTU	South African Congress of Trade Unions
SCS	Swiss Bank Corporation
SEG	Staff Executive Group
SWAPO	South-West African People's Organization
TRC	Truth and Reconciliation Commission
UBS	Union Bank of Switzerland
UNCTAD	United Nations Conference on Trade and Development
UNHCR	United Nationl High Commissioner for Refugees
UNITA	National Union for the Total Independence of Angola
WARC	World Alliance of Reformed Churches
WCC	World Council of Churches
WSCF	World Student Christian Federation
WUS	World University Service
YMCA	Young Men's Christian Association
YWCA	Young Women's Christian Association

1. Utrecht, 1953–1956

Beginnings

I was born in 1927 in Rotterdam, in between two world wars and just before the infamous crash of the New York Stock Exchange in 1929, which made many millions of people all over the world jobless. I would become aware of this much later. Mine was a privileged family, and we enjoyed the benefits of it. The economic crisis was never discussed in front of me or my younger brother, Bernard.

The origins of the Sjollema family – mostly teachers – are in Friesland, which, like Scotland, in the past aspired to becoming independent. My grandfather (and godfather), Bouwe Sjollema, was the last in our family to speak Frisian. He was proud of his background and loved to sing the Frisian national anthem to us!

Nothing in my young life predicted that I would be active in a church, let alone that I would become involved in church or ecumenical work. My parents and grandparents were liberals. My mother's family were Huguenots who migrated to the Netherlands in the 17th century; they belonged to the French-speaking Reformed Church in

Holland, in which I was baptized. But I never went to Sunday school. Every now and then, my mother would read us stories from the children's Bible – as part of our education, we had to know what the Bible was about. But that was it. My father wanted me to study law and succeed him as a lawyer.

But the Second World War changed our outlook. The German invasion of the Netherlands in 1940, the air raids that destroyed my home town Rotterdam, and the Nazi occupation of five long and difficult years led many Dutch people to actively or passively resist the brutal Nazi regime. Parliament was dissolved, political parties and trade unions were banned, and the media were censored. Political life came to a standstill. We were governed by a German *Reichskommissar* appointed by Hitler. Queen Wilhelmina and her government fled to London; she became our national symbol, but she was far away from our daily struggle to survive.

Thus the role of the church was significant. It provided one of the few forums for free discussion, although we always had to be careful: *der Feind hört mit*, the enemy is always listening. Many more people than usual were eager to hear the message from the pulpit of our churches. For some, and certainly for me, Bible study became a significant instrument in resisting the racist Nazi ideology, particularly when anti-Semitism was legalized.

The Jews became outcasts; they were systematically persecuted and sent to Auschwitz. But it was not only the Jews who were the target of the Nazis: all those who openly resisted and refused to cooperate were in danger of being arrested and deported. In this situation, the churches spoke out regularly and clearly on several occasions and showed solidarity with the discriminated. What was said from the pulpit was no longer theoretical: it related to daily life. This struck me as something very important. Not much later – in May 1945, the very day the Canadian troops liberated Rotterdam – my future wife and I were both confirmed and became active members of the Netherlands Reformed Church.

Resistance against oppression and solidarity with the discriminated would become and remain guiding principles in my life. And as time went on, other crucial questions also preoccupied me: What do liberation and freedom really mean? How can we be reconciled with "the enemy"? And how can we break the endless chain of revenge that haunts our different histories? There were no ready-made answers. But during my ecumenical involvement, I became aware of at least some of the elements that matter.

The challenge to be part of the ecumenical movement became even more pressing when I heard Martin Niemöller speak at a youth rally in Amsterdam in 1946. He was well-known and admired in Holland as a German who had dared to oppose the Nazis and who had been made to pay for his outspokenness by years in a concentration camp. What he had to say struck me as genuine. He not only apologized and repented for what his fellow country people had done to the rest of Europe; he also made a sharp analysis of the post-war situation and called for young people of different nations and confessions to face the issues that lay ahead and to avoid another war through an unambiguous joint ecumenical involvement. His appeal did not fall on deaf ears! Two years later, Jet, my future wife and companion, and I together attended one of the public sessions of the first assembly of the World Council of Churches (WCC) in Amsterdam in 1948. What I saw and heard there awoke in me a passion to become part of the ecumenical movement "somehow and somewhere."

But for that I had to prepare myself. The wish to go in a different direction from what my father expected of me became clear only at the end of my military service in 1950. I switched from law studies to sociology at the University of Utrecht, and from that point on I never looked back.

In 1953, when I left the University of Utrecht (provisionally: I returned in 1967 to complete my masters in sociology), the post–Second World War reconstruction process in the Netherlands had been largely completed. The country had suffered badly from the Nazi occupation, but thanks to the enthusiasm and energy that characterized the generation of our parents – who were then in their forties – the nation had regained its economic and social strength. However, it was going through a major political crisis that was to have long-term consequences.

The end of the war signalled the beginning of a worldwide process of decolonization after the Japanese defeat and surrender in 1945. The Netherlands was the third biggest colonial power in the world. The people of Indonesia (Dutch East Indies) were fighting for their independence, but the Dutch were not ready for a transfer of power. Theirs was a brutal and misguided military effort, involving some 150,000 Dutch soldiers in a so-called police action. For obvious political reasons, there was never any mention of a "war," which is what it really was. Finally, the Dutch were forced by Indonesian freedom fighters and under pressure from the UN to abandon colonial rule and to hand over sovereignty to the Indonesians. The Dutch government had misread the signs of the times. Indonesia proclaimed its independence on 17 August 1945, but it took until 1949, after much bloodshed and loss of life, for the Dutch to accept an official transfer of power.

Just before we married in 1953, the WCC informed me that I could apply for a job with Dutch interchurch aid and service to refugees in Utrecht. That was not really what I wanted. My strong desire had been to work somewhere with refugees in Africa, *away* from Holland. The idea grew when I spent a short time working in Munich in the summer of 1951 as part of my sociology studies in Utrecht. Two Dutch friends of mine – Jan van Hoogstraten, whom I knew from a Student Christian Movement camp during the war, and Ton van der Burg, both working with the World University Service (WUS) – had told me of the possibility of a job with WUS for a couple of months in a refugee camp near Munich. This appealed to me. I lived in a house with other refugee field workers and had my own car with US license plates, because at that time Munich was in the American-occupied zone of Germany.

Assisting Dutch Indonesians migrating to the US

I started my job in the Dutch interchurch aid office on 1 December 1953, immediately following my honeymoon. The director was Oncko Heldring. He and his wife, Lucy, quickly became very good friends and I could not have had a better and more interesting and intelligent first employer. I had been told that I was to assist the director, but when I asked him whether it wouldn't be a good idea to go through the pile of his unanswered mail, he said smilingly, "No, don't worry, just leave it there, those letters will answer themselves in three months' time!" From that I concluded that I would have to invent my own job description, and for a short while I helped to resettle some White Russian refugees, victims of communism.

However, early in 1954 the WCC (with whom I had already been in touch earlier regarding the White Russians) asked me to be their resettlement officer for refugees and deal with applicants for emigration to the US among the more than 200,000 Dutch Indonesians who were repatriated to Holland after Indonesian independence. Most of them had been born in Indonesia (including some 15,000 South Moluccans who had served in the Dutch colonial army). Many had at least one parent of Indonesian descent.

The majority of the Dutch colonial settlers had been prisoners in Japanese concentration camps during the war, and returning to their home country was an emotional experience for them. But for those of Indonesian origin – and they were the great majority – the evacuation was traumatic. They had Dutch nationality, and thus they were not considered to be refugees as such. The Dutch government and the general public in Holland believed there would be an "invisible integration" of these people into Dutch society. But the "repatriates" felt differently. They considered themselves victims not only of the Japanese occupation but also of decolonization. They received a lukewarm reception and felt they were discriminated against by the authorities. There were no signs of acknowledgment of their past or of the significant contribution they had made to colonial rule. They felt like second-class citizens in Dutch society and demanded some form of recognition and compensation. They had served their Dutch colonial masters and now saw no future in a newly independent Indonesia since they were afraid of being treated – and with some reason – as traitors by the Soekarno regime. But after they arrived in Holland they soon found out that the climate there was cold in every respect: not only geographically but also culturally, politically, and socially. They were in fact refugees and thus a burden.

On a more personal note, I should add that my mother, as national president of the Dutch Union of Women Volunteers, was co-responsible with the Dutch Red Cross for the reception, on arrival by boat in Rotterdam, of the Dutch Indonesians, most of whom had never been in Holland before. They were given clothes, food, and a first welcome before being bussed to reception centres all over the country. My job – at the request of the WCC – was to help large numbers of these same people to leave Holland and to emigrate to the US. So in a sense my mother and I were both involved in the aftermath of colonialism and concerned with helping its victims. In fact, my maternal great-great grandfather, Frederik s' Jacob, had been governor-general of the Dutch East Indies (1881-84) and thus was the highest Dutch colonial authority, though only for a brief period. For centuries, the lives of many Dutch families were intimately connected with the East Indies, through civil administration, commerce, and the military, as well as politically and through the Christian missions. Many fortunes were made there, in the sugar, coffee, and tea plantations or in the oil industry (Royal Dutch Shell).

The hurdles

It was understandable that some of the more enterprising among these Dutch Indonesians wanted to emigrate elsewhere, and a chance came up under the US Refugee Relief Act. In February 1953, following floods that ravaged much of the agriculture in the south-western part of the Netherlands, the US government agreed to include, in its

Refugee Relief Act, a special category for these flood victims. The US needed farmers and thought this was an occasion not to be missed. However, only a few victims were interested, and the quota of 15,000 remained largely unfilled. The Dutch government seized the opportunity and negotiated with Washington the inclusion in their stead of Dutch Indonesian repatriates. And thanks to the determined efforts of US Senator Francis Walter, this effort largely succeeded.

Thousands of Dutch Indonesians desiring to leave registered at the American consulate-general in Rotterdam. But many of them were of mixed Asian-European blood. So here was another hurdle: most immigration countries, and in particular Australia, Canada, and the US, had white immigration policies and strict selection criteria. In the end, though, some 50,000 managed to emigrate, and about a third of those went to the US.

Before they were allowed to leave for the US, however, they needed an affidavit of support in that country, a job, and a financial guarantee for the first year. Church congregations in the US were willing to provide these affidavits on the basis of a detailed dossier. Thus I had to interview each family and decide whether they would be able to integrate into American society. But nobody in the US had any idea what kind of people "Dutch Indonesians" might be.

In order to gain a better understanding myself about that vast country, I was sent to the US for a couple of weeks in June-July 1955, just before the birth of our eldest daughter, Suzanne. I sailed from Rotterdam on the *MS Waterman* together with hundreds of Dutch emigrants to Canada. In order to pay my passage, I was supposed to organize information sessions on life in Canada. As I didn't know much about the country, I was more than happy that soon after departure a storm broke out and most people were sea-sick until the end of the voyage! It did not affect me too much, but most people stayed in their cabin for the rest of the trip and my counselling was no longer needed. We stopped in Halifax, where most emigrants went ashore. From there we sailed on to New York on an almost empty ship. During the trip I made acquaintance with the chaplain on board, who happened to be the son-in-law of Dr W.A. Visser 't Hooft, general secretary of the WCC. Like me, Mario Musacchio had little to do, and we had a good time together discussing the ecumenical movement.

My stay in the US was quite interesting. My programme was set up by Jan Van Hoogstraten who then worked for Church World Service (CWS) in New York, the refugee programme of the US council of churches. I was sent to the mid-west, Iowa and Michigan; had numerous meetings with Americans, many of Dutch descent; and had to "preach" (give a message) in church services and to "sell" Dutch Indonesians families. This was not always easy, because people wanted to know – discreetly, of course – whether these people were white or Asian. In one case, I talked about a bar-keeper and the congregation was interested, thinking our barman was a *milk*bar man – "no alcohol in our community"! Well, I told them he was just that, and once back in Holland I told the man that from now on he was a milk-shaker and he would have to prepare himself for that job accordingly if he wanted to stand a chance. Which, incidentally, is what he did – and he got the job.

My return to Holland was quite different. I was booked by the Dutch government as its guest on the modern and beautiful tourist liner *MS Maasdam*, a flagship of the Holland-America Line, of which my grandfather, Frederik s' Jacob, had been a director (1922-33). I was given a VIP cabin next to the captain on the highest deck. To my surprise, on arrival in Rotterdam – the journey took five days – several journalists were waiting for me, all anxious to report how many sponsors I had found in the US. And since I had been rather successful, contrary to other NGOs who had gone before me, I got some headlines in local and national newspapers.

The procedures

In a normal working day, not only in Utrecht but all over Holland, I called up and interviewed about seven or eight persons or families, a procedure that was tiring but interesting because of their stories. For some, it was clear from the outset that the person was still living so much in his or her colonial past that chances of resettlement in the US had to be considered slim. I had to tell them I was unable to help them – obviously not an easy message to convey.

In one case I interviewed an elderly man, who thought he could leave his wife in the waiting room while he himself insisted on standing in front of me, clearly thinking in colonial terms that I was his master. It took me quite a while to explain that he would not fit into American society.

For each person, a dossier was established and sent to the WCC in Geneva to be studied and forwarded to Church World Service in New York. In turn, CWS sent these dossiers to different churches in the US for sponsorship. In Utrecht we regularly received the visit of US church officials who wanted to meet and interview applicants themselves. That proved very helpful, as they took a personal interest in getting people placed back home. It also meant that Jet and I had to entertain them, which was pleasant but time-consuming and sometimes complicated because our children Suzanne and Inge were still very young. The job also involved developing close relations with the Dutch government department responsible for emigration, and not least with the American consulate-general in Rotterdam.

But there was one big obstacle with the Americans: the question of having to prove that Dutch Indonesians were more than 50 percent white ("Caucasian"). This we refused from the beginning, and I made this clear on behalf of the WCC to the American consul-general. We could and would never indulge in a racist game because it was contrary to our faith and to the policies of the WCC. After a while the Americans stopped asking. The Dutch government in turn succeeded in having the refugees identified as "ethnic Dutch," which more or less solved the race issue, at least on paper.

As work increased, I needed qualified help for the interviews and the administration, and I appointed Jan Möhringer, who had been educated in the US (Moody Bible School) and who knew the situation there quite well. Later on Bill Allard joined us: he had worked with the YMCA. We became close friends and he provided considerable support (just as the Hungarian revolution started and Hungarian refugees poured into Austria, WCC Geneva recruited him to become its chief resettlement officer in Salzburg).

Fortunately, the WCC in Geneva was fully responsible for the resettlement budget in the Utrecht office. In the end we needed four people to do the work. In about five years (which went beyond my time as the responsible person for the WCC operation in Holland), out of a total of 15,000 persons we helped to resettle some 3000-4000 in the US. Nearly all of them wanted to go to California because of the climate, but that was not possible, at least not initially. Most congregations and parishes volunteering to sponsor Dutch-Indonesians were on the east coast or in the mid-west. But after a year in the US, the refugees were on their own and they could move westward on their own initiative.

Meanwhile, research on the integration of these people has shown that most of the migrants settled successfully. They moved up the social ladder quickly, in spite of the fact that their diplomas were not recognized in the United States. About one-third were able to buy a house within five years. None disappeared into ethnic ghettos. One of the reasons for this positive development seems to have been the support they received from the sponsoring congregations. Fears about racist behaviour on the part of the receiving communities were clearly unfounded. Most immigrants lost their Indonesian traditions and accepted "the American way of life," although it was also reported that Dutch-Indonesians in California – like other ethnic groups – frequently created their own social clubs.

My three years in Utrecht were an interesting and instructive period. I was on my own and had to improvise, but I also found myself moving in Dutch emigration circles with a much longer history than the WCC. Although I was their junior, it so happened that the WCC and its partner Church World Service in the US were much more successful in finding sponsors than all the other organizations with a similar aim, including the Roman Catholics. This sometimes created tensions with my senior colleagues in other agencies.

Occasionally I went to report to Geneva, where I got to know the worldwide WCC refugee resettlement staff, notably Edgar Chandler, its director, and Margaret Jaboor, his deputy, a stern and hard-working Scottish woman, who did most of the day-to-day work. She would telephone me at least twice a week to find out how our work was going.

In 1954, I attended a WCC fraternal workers retreat organized by Ken Baker at the Ecumenical Institute, Bossey, near Geneva, and was greatly impressed by the Bible studies led by Suzanne de Dietrich, a small woman who, despite her severe physical handicap, spoke with great authority. Her passion for life combined with a passion for reading the Bible critically was an eye-opener: the Bible suddenly became related to daily life and to history. I was also impressed by the fact that she listened intensely and that she was open to our questions – she was not the usual theologian defending certain theories or dogmas. In fact, she was a lay woman, trained as an engineer, and as a biblicist she had a keen interest in making us discover the Bible stories for ourselves. During that retreat, together with other participants I began to discover the meaning of the word *oikoumene* as the whole inhabited world and not just the unity of the churches. This proved of crucial importance for my future ecumenical understanding and involvement.

But at that Bossey retreat I also encountered, for the first time since the war, committed Christians from Germany, and this confronted me with the question of reconciliation. Was it possible to be reconciled with the Germans? And what would it take? In May 1940 they had invaded our country and after five days the Dutch were forced to surrender. The Luftwaffe bombed and destroyed large areas of my home town, Rotterdam – a terrible experience. Fortunately, we as a family were spared, but the scars of that war and the five-year occupation (1940-45) by the Nazis remained. All the more so as the only brother of my mother, a reserve officer in the Dutch army, had been killed by the Nazis. The war had meant untold hardship, and many people had taken an active part in the resistance movement. Nazism was an evil racist system, responsible for killing millions of people all over Europe. It was especially responsible for the Shoah.

But at Bossey I was confronted not by a system but by German people of my age – I was then 27 years old. They struggled with a horrible legacy, and they were a generation anxious to listen and be forgiven. It became a genuine encounter between persons opening up to each other and trying to come to terms with the past. What was essential and quite new for me was to realize how much many ordinary Germans, too, had suffered and been the victims of the same diabolical system. For me, our meeting at Bossey was an important beginning on the way to reconciliation.

Later, in the 1960s and 1970s when I was a Geneva WCC staff member, German colleagues – Werner Simpfendorfer and Ulrich Becker – were among my best friends and reconciliation became concrete, but not before long discussions and my coming to understand their own suffering at the hands of the Nazis.

At the end of 1956, just before leaving for my next job in Vienna, I went for a couple of days to Taizé in France on a personal retreat under the supervision of Frère Max Thurian. Taizé was small at that time and the services were still held in the original small village church. I found it difficult to submit to the discipline of the order, and especially to the austere character of Frère Max, who later converted to Roman Catholicism. But it was an experience I would remember: the silence and the spirituality of the place and of its brothers, the time for meditation, and the beautiful landscape of Burgundy.

2. Vienna, 1957-1958

Looking back, 1956 was a turning point for me in several respects. First, it was the year when the UK, France, and Israel unilaterally launched their invasion of Egypt in order to gain control of the Suez Canal. Predictably, the US categorically refused any responsibility for the intervention and the USSR threatened "massive reprisals." By the end of the year, all the invading troops had left Egypt – the operation had turned into a catastrophic failure. For the two former colonial powers this meant the end of their hegemony in the region, and marked a further step in the worldwide decolonization process.

The Hungarian revolution

But 1956 was also a turning-point in the history of another part of the world. On October 23, a group of demonstrators in Budapest clashed with Hungarian police. It was the beginning of what would become the Hungarian revolution. What happened was something we had not imagined possible in our life-time: a first dent in the communist bulwark of Eastern Europe. Imre Nagy, a communist reformer ("socialism with a human face"), formed a new government. He courageously announced the end of one-party rule and the withdrawal of Hungary from the Warsaw Pact. It was a spontaneous national movement of opposition by students, factory workers, and intellectuals, among whom were many communists. They protested not only against Stalinism but also against capitalism. Innumerable local revolutionary committees were formed. The Hungarian uprising proved to be a moment of truth in history. What happened there in 1956 was to be the first revolution against the Stalinist regime of the Soviet Union. In fact, we were faced with the question of whether this was a revolution confined to Hungary and other parts of Eastern Europe or whether it concerned us in the West as well.

In this context, it is interesting to note that in 1989, 33 years after the Hungarian revolution, Imre Nagy was rehabilitated by the Hungarian supreme court and reburied in Budapest as a national hero. Heroes Square was bedecked with huge red, white, and green flags, each with a hole cut out where the communist insignia used to be, as had been done in 1956. One Hungarian historian spoke about "the victory of a defeat." And even a defeat can be a milestone on the road to change.

The uprising was short-lived: it lasted only 12 days. Nikita Khrushchev and the members of the communist praesidium decided to crush the revolution on November 4. The Soviet army launched a harsh repression, and by November 20, all resistance had ended. TV images of the bloody street fighting in Budapest showed the courage of heroic Hungarian resistance fighters and the cruelty of the Soviet troops. More than 3000 Hungarians died and some 20,000 were wounded, and these figures don't include the hundreds of summary executions by the Soviets. Nagy was arrested and sentenced to death.

What happened in those days destroyed my idealistic dreams of a socialist-Marxist society. The West didn't intervene and the Hungarians felt betrayed, especially since for years they had heard Voice of America and Radio Free Europe calling them to rise up against communism.

There was a fear that this might be the beginning of further Soviet threats, this time to the West. How far would the Soviets go? And above all, what would the US do? These were very alarming thoughts at the time. But we were forgetting that the Cold War still had strong spheres of influence in both camps, which did not yet allow for a change in the status quo. The US made it known to the USSR that events in Hungary were considered an internal matter within the Soviet bloc. Consequently, it would not intervene. Prudence was the watchword.

Dealing with the aftermath

Unexpectedly, the events in Hungary would influence my own future and that of my family. I received an urgent invitation from the WCC to go to Vienna. I had to decide within 48 hours whether I wanted to be involved in the resettling of some of the 200,000 victims of the revolution who were fleeing to Austria. In spite of anxieties about being left with the children in Holland, at least for a couple of months, my wife Jet encouraged me to accept. After three years in Utrecht, I was in fact ready to move. And so I accepted, though not without some fears, given my lack of experience, of moving to an unknown environment outside my own culture. Originally, I had wanted to go to Africa, but moving near to the borders of communist Eastern Europe was enough of a challenge for a start!

Early in January 1957, I left Utrecht by night train and arrived the next day in Vienna. The city was still in a state of emergency. Hundreds of Hungarians had been entering every day and needed shelter. The Austrian government had been accustomed to helping refugees from communist countries since the end of the Second World War, but not on this scale. It had to improvise transport, housing, medical, and other services. It had to decentralize the refugees, but it could not avoid large numbers staying in Vienna. For ten years the city had been divided into four zones of occupation: American, British, French, and Soviet, which only ended in 1955. The Viennese had only just started to enjoy their re-won freedom (Hitler had annexed Austria in 1938) when the Hungarian revolution became a major challenge to Austria's capacity, as a newly independent country, to receive refugees.

As part of its Cold-War policies, the West – and in particular the Americans – set up extensive aid programmes to help the victims of communism; and Austria, among others, benefited considerably from this. So did the NGOs assisting refugees, including the WCC, which received a per capita grant from the US State Department in Washington, DC, for each refugee family from a communist country resettled overseas. The fact that this was not simply a humanitarian operation but was also part of US anti-communist Cold-War policy angered me quite a bit, but on the positive side special refugee laws made it possible for many Hungarians to resettle in the US, Australia, Canada, and New Zealand. Western Europe also received its share. The many international NGOs helping refugees provided sponsors in immigration countries. As for the WCC, on the basis of a dossier for each family, it found church congregations in other continents opening their doors and showing generous hospitality.

Directing WCC's Vienna refugee office

I was appointed director of the Vienna area office, responsible for the WCC's operations in Vienna. My superior was Arthur Foster, director for the whole of Austria. His office was in Salzburg, but he would come to Vienna regularly (and would stay, as I did, in the beginning, in the Hotel Astoria) for meetings and to glean first-hand information. I had a good relationship with him, and he gave me a free hand in most matters.

In 1956, the WCC already had a very small refugee office in Vienna. But the Hungarian crisis made it necessary to overhaul its size and organization completely. When I arrived I quickly understood that we had to find other more adequate premises. This was what "Geneva" expected of me: To make a plan to deal with a constant stream of people arriving daily and asking to be registered for emigration overseas. The Austrian government made it clear it could house them only temporarily and was counting on other countries to resettle them permanently. Initially, many Hungarians wanted to stay in Austria, believing they could soon return home. In a matter of weeks I appointed some twenty staff members, partly Austrian, partly refugees from earlier days. We needed translators, secretaries, accountants, and interviewers who could explain the legislation of different immigration countries.

I found a small house in Pötzleinsdorf and three months after my arrival, Jet followed. Some furniture arrived from Holland. My mother, together with an "au pair," brought our two children, Suzanne and Inge (respectively one and a half years and six months old). Our parents, brothers, and sisters invited themselves, as everybody wanted to see Vienna and go to the opera!

Our new offices on Dr Karl Luegerring Street were on the fourth floor, in a building with a very old elevator that broke down frequently. Climbing the stairs made things particularly difficult for families with small children and for elderly people, but that was part of life in Vienna. We appointed a Hungarian at the reception to meet newcomers and direct them to the appropriate desk. His name was Geza Bacsi ("uncle"), a fatherly man who was getting on a bit and who had once worked in a circus. Everybody loved him, but of course refugees tried to take advantage of his friendly nature by asking for preferential treatment.

After nine months I was informed by Geneva that financial problems required cuts in staff. This proved to be the most difficult decision I had to make during my time in Vienna. Everyone was working hard, doing overtime and dedicated to the cause. We had become friends, not just colleagues. After long hesitation, I decided to tell Geza Bacsi that he was one of those who would have to leave. When he came into my office, I asked him to sit down. But he refused, saying that he couldn't do so in front of his director. When I had finished explaining with a lot of pain why he would have to go, he stared at me and then said in a trembling voice: "Aber Herr Direktor, Ich war doch immer Ihr treuer Hund..." (Literally, "But, Mr Director, I have always been your faithful dog.") This touched me so much that I didn't have the courage to continue the discussion. So I reconsidered his case. There was of course no rationale in my reasoning this way. His reaction reflected the culture of the old Austro-Hungarian empire in which he had been brought up and which in many ways was still very much part of life in Vienna at that time. In a way he embodied something I liked about the Austrians and Hungarians: their politeness. In any event, I couldn't resist Geza Bacsi and a couple of days later I told him he could stay. He bowed deeply and left my office without saying a word. Later on I was told that he was kept long after I had left, and that he died while still employed by the office.

Another time, when I was alone in the office on a Saturday morning trying to get rid of a backlog, there was a knock on my door and in came a distressed and highly nervous Hungarian couple. They asked me to help them find a place to hide urgently. It turned out that they and their children had emigrated to the US a couple of months earlier with the help of our office. But one morning very early the FBI knocked at their door and told them they would be deported because it had been established that the husband had been spying in Austria for the Hungarian communist regime before fleeing to Vienna in 1956. They were immediately flown back to Vienna, and he rightly feared that the Austrian authorities might arrest and try him. I consulted a colleague from the refugee office of the Lutheran World Service. Fortunately, she was very pragmatic and organized for the family to be sheltered in a Lutheran old people's home in a suburb of Vienna.

I remained regularly in touch with the father, who went through several periods of depression. But the family "made it." They remained in Austria and in the end became Austrian citizens. Later, when their youngest son was born, they asked me to become his godfather and he was baptized in the Reformed Church by our friend and pastor Sascha Abrahamowicz. My godson and I developed a close friendship after his father died in 1990. He also became an Austrian citizen and is now lecturer at the University of Klagenfurt, where he lives with his wife and children, a delightful couple whom we visited in 2005 and with whom we went to Budapest in 2006 to be shown around the home town of his parents. This was particularly important for me, as I wanted to get a feeling of Hungarian history and see some of the historical places related to the revolution of 1956.

But then, in the middle of 1957, I received a letter from the WCC asking me to move to Geneva to take responsibility for a two-year study and conference on "International Migration and the Responsibility of the Churches." I first objected on the grounds that I had only just started my work in Vienna and did not want to change so quickly. But after more pressure and further thought, I accepted. The flow of refugees by that time had considerably slowed down and made the Geneva offer more attractive. And so we left Austria – not without a certain feeling of "home-sickness" – at the end of December of the same year we had arrived.

3. Geneva, 1958-1981

I arrived in Geneva on 4 January 1958, thinking I would find busy offices and a lot of new colleagues. In fact, the offices were empty. I didn't know, and nobody had told me, that staff of international organizations in Geneva usually take a long Christmas leave!

I must confess that I was somewhat disappointed in my high expectations of the new job. Correspondence with the WCC about my appointment in Geneva had been confused. My title was Migration Study Secretary, but the assignment was very vague. Also, I received no clear answer to my repeated questions about my salary. In the end, Frank Northam, the treasurer, wrote that the matter would be decided once I arrived in Geneva. I nevertheless decided to accept, because I continued to trust my employers completely.

The WCC's Malagnou campus consisted of four villas and three wooden barracks, housing some 150 staff. The Lutheran World Federation occupied one of these buildings. I was assigned a small, dark office on the top floor in the same building as the refugee service, by far the biggest WCC activity, having offices all over the world (the Vienna office was part of it).

I tried to find out what was expected of me. I had been appointed as the result of a decision taken by the WCC central committee in Galyatetö (Hungary) in late 1956, just before the Hungarian revolution. But there was no detailed job description and neither of my two superiors, Leslie Cooke and Elfan Rees, could fill me in with any great detail. They agreed that the distinction between refugees and migrants made in the early post-war years was rapidly becoming obsolete due to events. The WCC itself had difficulty in distinguishing its services between refugees on the move and migrants in need. It had a mandate from the churches to serve refugees but none for service to migrants, and no such ministry was planned by the churches themselves. An international conference on migration was to be organized on the basis of a two-year study, and an international preparatory commission needed to be appointed to oversee progress and decide on the venue and the substance of the conference programme.

As I found out only later, the idea of this study originated in the WCC's service to refugees, which in recent years had been the best-known and the best funded part of the WCC. This was thanks to, among other things, the per capita grants from the US government for refugees from communist countries in Eastern Europe (Edgar Chandler, the director of the WCC's Service to Refugees, was an American).

Hans Lilje, the Lutheran bishop of Hanover and a member of the WCC central committee, proposed a study on migration and the responsibility of the churches, and his resolution was adopted. But by the time I arrived in Geneva one year later to implement the resolution, money for the refugee service was no longer plentiful. In fact, the service was running a deficit and there was little likelihood of it expanding as a result of the migration study. Consequently, interest was waning but the central committee resolution was still on the books, and even if the WCC itself was now no longer likely to get involved directly in a service to migrants, the broader issue of the churches' responsibility in this field remained valid.

Guidance in "the language of heaven"!

This development within the WCC resulted in contradictory advice from my two supervisors as to how to carry out my mandate. I found myself in the uncomfortable position of having to cope with two bosses who didn't see eye to eye.

When I confronted Leslie Cooke with the problem, he suggested that I go and see "le patron," the general secretary Dr Willem A. Visser 't Hooft, and ask for his advice. "You had better go and talk the language of heaven with him," as Cooke put it (Visser 't Hooft was Dutch, like me)! He also told me how to prepare for an interview with him and what to expect when phoning him for a date: You ring him in the morning, said Leslie, and he will tell you that he has no time to see you then, but will ring you back in the afternoon for an appointment. Be sure to expect the call sharply at two o'clock and he will ask you to come at once. And this is exactly how it happened! Cooke also warned me that I was to prepare my questions in a clear and logical manner – no nonsense! – and not to take any notes during the meeting.

And so a couple of months after I arrived in Geneva, I ran with high hopes from one building to another to see *"le patron."* I was quite nervous, as most colleagues were rather scared of him because of his sharp mind and stern character. I had met Visser 't Hooft only once or twice at tea time (the daily moment when all staff meet informally), so I didn't know him well. As I entered his office in the old villa at Malagnou, I saw the sharp profile of the man sitting behind an enormous old wooden desk, his face clearly visible between huge loads of files and books on either side. He kindly invited me to sit down in one of the two leather armchairs: its springs were evidently worn out, for I sank almost to the floor. From there I looked up to him as if to God in heaven – in any case, I felt an enormous distance between the two of us. He asked me what I wanted and I rattled off my questions: I told him what I had understood the task to be, and that neither Cooke nor Rees were clear about the mandate for my work, and that in any case it was impossible to have two bosses. Once I had finished my litany, he stood and paced up and down the room for what seemed to me hours. Finally, he sat down next to me in the other chair and suddenly we were on the same level. Well, he said – in the language of heaven! – you should look at this migration study, and at yourself for that matter, as being a tiny little part of the diamond that is the ecumenical movement. And as you turn that diamond around you will see precious new aspects each time. In other words, you are only part, totally interdependent with other parts. You have to look at migration as being intimately related to other issues, such as the mission of the church, evangelism, the role of the laity, interchurch aid, relations with other faiths, and let's not forget the socio-economic and demographic developments in different parts of the world. Then, with his sharp mind, he formulated a series of issues to be explored in view of the conference I was to organize, and indicated that he himself would chair a staff group to supervise and guide my work and that I should report regularly to him.

For the first time since I had arrived in Geneva, I felt I was doing something worthwhile and had received the necessary guidance. But most importantly, I felt I was part of the movement and had my own distinct contribution to make. When I went back to Leslie Cooke and Elfan Rees to report on the results of my conversation, I was all the happier since Rees had treated me very much as his junior colleague and considered the migration study very much as "his baby." I felt relieved that the ambiguity of my work situation had been resolved and that Visser 't Hooft had taken the lead. I couldn't have expected more!

Portrait of the WCC's first general secretary

Willem Visser 't Hooft (1900-85) was not an easy boss for his colleagues: very challenging, a bit shy, stern, and Calvinistic, but at the same time pastoral in crisis situations (as we experienced when we lost our eldest daughter Suzanne in 1963 in an accident). He was always several steps ahead of his colleagues on the issues they wanted to discuss. And there was never small talk.

One day at tea-time at Malagnou, my colleagues, Lukas Vischer and Albert van den Heuvel, and I tackled him on a book about the ecumenical movement that had just appeared. The three of us had decided that each of us would read a part of the book. We were as excited as small boys and were sure that he wouldn't have read it yet. When we had each made our short introductions, he kept quiet for a moment and then said, with a twinkle in his eye, "Yes, you are right, it is an interesting book, but you forgot to mention something essential in chapter. . . ."

Some believed he was more a general than a secretary! I would call him a visionary and the architect behind the WCC's becoming the privileged instrument of the ecumenical movement. Very demanding and sharp in his analysis, he was not only a theologian but a statesman as well. His concern was about the churches in relation to what happened in the world: how the unity of the churches could contribute to the unity of humankind, rather than only how Christians could unite for their own sake. Unity was always seen as a condition for a possible contribution to justice and peace in the world at large. He was a man with the Bible in one hand and a newspaper in the other, as Karl Barth had taught him and us as well. His theology was a biblical theology, Christ-centred: Bible studies were essential in order to discover what God is asking from us and how to respond to his call. Visser 't Hooft read several newspapers daily, and the story was that by 8:30 A.M. when we arrived at work, he had already finished reading *Le Monde*.

Relations with the Roman Catholic Church became a crucial issue, especially during and after the Second Vatican Council. And when Pope Paul VI visited the WCC in 1969 in its new building, the question of possible Roman Catholic membership in the WCC was considered for the first time. But only for a short while, to Visser 't Hooft's great sadness, because Rome had never really taken membership seriously.

Visser 't Hooft became increasingly wary about cooperating with other religions and often warned about the danger of syncretism. In

1963 he wrote a book entitled *No Other Name*, which clearly underlined that Jesus Christ is the only name of humankind's salvation. "Every time Christians use the word *religion* meaning something wider than Christianity, but including Christianity, they contribute to the syncretistic mood of our times and strengthen the conviction that the truly universal force is religion, not Christianity."[1] And "there must be no compromise of any kind. We cannot participate in the search for a common denominator of all the religions..."[2] His thinking was closely linked to Karl Barth's Christocentric view that only an encounter with God and response to God's initiative in Christ can bring salvation to human beings. There is "no other name" by which people could be saved. Barth had an enormous impact on that generation of ecumenical leaders. But eventually, people like D.T. Niles and others nuanced their positions to accommodate new social and political realities and the growing need to respond to other religions in the post-colonial world. Not long after Visser 't Hooft's death in 1985, the WCC was to engage in dialogue with other religions, which gradually became an essential part of the council's life.

Visser 't Hooft always concentrated on what he considered the essence of an issue. He would come into the middle of a meeting, listen for a while, and then make a remark or raise a question that usually went right to the heart of the matter but was often being neglected by those present. But before you could realize how foolish you felt, he had already left for another meeting!

After his retirement, Visser 't Hooft remained very visible. He continued to have an office in the WCC where he would be every afternoon, and he had his "own" table at tea-time in the cafeteria. He "received" people at his table and was much consulted. Although his successor, Eugene Blake, had agreed that he should keep an office in the WCC, his presence became understandably somewhat embarrassing to Blake.

Visser 't Hooft also initiated a study group, meeting one evening a month at his home. Some fifteen or more colleagues would attend, and it was felt to be quite an honour if you belonged to the group. He himself or one of the participants would introduce a subject. Afterwards, we were entitled to a glass of wine. One evening I broke a crystal glass and felt ashamed. Since it was near St Nicolas day (December 5) I decided to give him a set of glasses to replace the broken one. I accompanied this with an anonymous poem, as is the St Nicolas tradition. A couple of days later, I received a beautiful poem back from him!

In 1971 Visser 't Hooft published his autobiography. I was then deeply involved in the Programme to Combat Racism and was of course particularly interested in what he had to say about his involvement in South Africa in the 1950-60s. He had indeed played a significant role, first by spending five weeks in the country in 1952.

Looking at that period of apartheid, it is clear that because of his Dutch background and his adherence to the Reformed confession, there was no one more suited to intervene, and especially to try and negotiate, with this very powerful, staunch, and hard-headed Reformed Afrikaner tribe. He listened carefully to them and asked penetrating questions about their calling as Christians in a racially divided country, adding that the central issue was to show the world that in Christ, these divisions were overcome. The time was still one of a serious attempt to come to mutual understanding through dialogue in order to find acceptable solutions. He never seemed to have used strong language in telling the Boers that time had run out and that the ecumenical family could no longer tolerate the South African churches' involvement and responsibility for the oppression of the black majority.

But nowhere, it seems, was there any sign that things would move toward a solution. In spite of Visser 't Hooft's questions to the churches, the tone of the conversations remained amicable. This is all the more amazing because he met several leaders of the African National Congress (ANC), among them Albert Luthuli, who later received the Nobel Peace Prize, and Z. K. Matthews who several years later would become WCC Africa secretary (it was he who taught me the history of the African liberation movement.). The ANC was already making it clear that after so many years, when non-violent methods of resistance had not resulted in any progress, their patience was running out.

Visser 't Hooft had a lasting influence on my way of working, and analyzing issues and seeing beyond today. He was one of the most remarkable ecumenical pioneers and I was lucky to serve several years under him. He had a good sense of humour, which he showed particularly at WCC Christmas parties, reading his limericks about the WCC's activities during the past year. Those were unforgettable moments! To me he was a kind of father figure. The younger generation of WCC staff members were rather afraid of him. The fact that we were both Dutch made my colleagues think I must have known him before joining the staff. In fact, as I mentioned earlier, I was introduced to him only several weeks after I arrived in Geneva.

Just a few months before Visser 't Hooft retired, he called me into his office and said he wanted to keep me on staff but I needed to finish my sociology studies. Of course I wanted to do that too, but I asked him how I could, with a family of four children and a job that demanded a lot of travelling. He looked at me and replied sternly, "Well, you should do as I did. I wrote my PhD at night." I was taken aback and said I would think about it. A few months later (in 1966), Eugene Blake, the new general secretary, took a different line: "I hear you want to have a sabbatical. I suspect you want to finish your studies at the WCC's expense and then move somewhere else for promotion." To which I replied that that was one way of looking at the issue. Another way would be to consider that I had already worked some ten years for the council and that a sabbatical would help me to better equip myself for any future work in WCC. That appealed to him and he decided to give me six months' paid leave as an incentive, and on presentation of favourable exam results, another six months leave, but this time without salary. And this is what happened. Eleven months later (at the end of 1967) I did my master's in sociology in Utrecht and was ready to serve another spell of duty with the WCC, not knowing what lay ahead.

Visser 't Hooft retired in 1966 and was made honorary president of the WCC. The choice of his successor led to a crisis. In 1963, the central committee in Rochester (instead of attending that meeting I should have participated in Martin Luther King's march on Washington and experience what the civil-rights movement was about!)

decided to entrust the nomination of Visser 't Hooft's successor to the executive committee And it did: it proposed as sole candidate Patrick Rodger, a Scottish Episcopalian on staff of the Faith and Order department. We were all surprised, not the least Visser 't Hooft himself, who had not been consulted. The general feeling was that he was a "light-weight" and had been chosen because the executive wanted more authority over policy matters after the long period of strong and sometimes unilateral leadership by Visser 't Hooft. The staff were very uneasy about this choice and started to lobby in support of a move among members of central committee to reconsider the executive's decision. A group of twenty colleagues circulated "strictly confidential and private" memos after we had individually been approached by members of the central committee. Visser 't Hooft clearly knew what was happening but didn't interfere, suggesting tacit approval of what we were doing. The 1965 central committee in Enugu decided to rescind its decision to appoint the executive committee as its nomination committee and appointed its own group, which then proposed Eugene Carson Blake, the Stated Clerk of the Presbyterian Church USA, a member of the executive committee.

Migration and migrant workers: A research job

After five years of action-oriented work in Utrecht and Vienna, constantly interviewing people and being responsible for a relatively big office with employees in Austria, I found it difficult to be confined to a study job in Geneva. Now, however, I had to find people who would contribute to thinking and writing on issues that were to be treated at the planned international conference. I tried to do that in consultation with the members of the preparatory commission. But to my regret their input was limited. So I concentrated on meeting people in the international organizations in Geneva (ILO, UNHCR, ICEM, and NGOs) involved in issues of migration and integration, and who would be aware of the human and sociological implications of the movement of people. But I soon discovered that many international civil servants were tied by (inter-) governmental policies and were little inclined to take the time to think freely and enter into real conversation on some of the basic issues in the context of migration that were our concern. Also, many in the UN and its agencies looked down on NGOs, and cooperation was not to be taken for granted.

Indicative of the lack of understanding of the study, even among some members on the commission, was the reaction by one member, Sir Stephen Holmes from the UK. At the end of the first meeting he stated, with an upper class accent, "I don't really understand what the problem is. Isn't there always an Anglican church around the corner?" This proved how little some of the elite really understood the problems for migrants of being uprooted and resettled. In hindsight, I feel very unhappy about the fact that we had no migrants on the commission – an omission we would not repeat later when I moved to the Programme to Combat Racism!

Progress on the study was slow. So I went to see Robert Mackie, who was chairperson of the preparatory commission as well as the chair of the WCC's division of interchurch aid and service to refugees. He listened patiently, then reassured me and strongly encouraged me to develop my own style and ideas. I felt relieved!

The main questions centred on identifying the causes of migration and the push-and-pull factors inciting potential migrants in the so-called developing countries to leave (push factors) and the attraction for them (pull factors) of developed economies in the West.

When the world conference on "Problems of International Migration and the Responsibility of the Churches" (11-16 June 1961, Leysin, Switzerland) finally opened, I sighed with relief. We had spent too much time in preparing for it. That was partly because, as I mentioned earlier, the momentum had been lost and colleagues were less interested, particularly since the financial situation of the service to refugees had deteriorated. But I realize now that it was also because I was not sufficiently aware of the thinking in other parts of the WCC. In particular, I would have found natural allies in the department on the laity, the youth department, the secretariat on racial and ethnic relations, as well as, following the WCC's third assembly in New Delhi in 1961, among those working on the study on the missionary structure of the congregation.

In spite of Visser 't Hooft's insistence at the beginning of the study that migration should never be looked at from an isolated perspective but always in the broader ecumenical context, in reality there was less cooperation and openness on the part of other sections of the WCC. Each desk or department had its own priorities as well as its constituency and historical context. And I probably did not insist sufficiently on the need for "in-house" discussions with other departments.

At the suggestion of Visser 't Hooft, I had asked Dr Franklin Clark Fry, chairperson of the WCC's central committee, to moderate the conference. That in itself gave the meeting a certain weight but also involved limitations. Fry had strong confessional loyalties. Visser 't Hooft was there too, but he was not very helpful when, an hour before the opening, he called out one of the key participants with whom I had worked closely, Jacques Beaumont (general secretary of Cimade, the ecumenical inter-movement committee for aid to evacuees in France) to go urgently to Lisbon to coordinate a rescue operation of some sixty Angolan and Mozambican students with scholarships from the Congregational and Methodist churches in the US, who were in danger of being arrested by the Portuguese secret service. [3]

In looking back at the results of the migration conference, I do not think it opened many new and exciting perspectives. As usual, there were more questions than answers. Many issues that I had hoped would be addressed were not really dealt with. My dream had been that the conference would meditate on the biblical understanding of hospitality: What is the fundamental meaning of hospitality to the stranger? By their very presence, strangers question our way of life, our codes of conduct, even pose a threat. Hospitality is closely linked to solidarity. It risks changing the life of both host and guest. These basic issues were barely touched on. They would, however, become some of the issues I would try to work on as the future secretary for migration in the WCC. On reflection, perhaps not much more could have been expected from the conference: a look at the list of participants and the leadership showed that this was a traditional meeting of church representatives. But nobody seemed committed to any far-reaching or exciting new ideas. The conference, not totally unexpectedly, recommended that the WCC should "discover the points at which ecumenical initiative on migration is called for, which might be provided by the WCC."[4]

The WCC's New Delhi assembly in 1961 then decided to create a secretariat for migration within the WCC's division of interchurch aid and service to refugees "in order that its guidance may be made available to the churches." This would include studies, counselling services, coordination of information, pilot projects, and expert representations at the inter-governmental level. A broad spectrum of initiatives could be put down on paper, but in practice, budgetary constraints allowed nothing more than an executive, a secretary, and a few small projects. The original dream of the WCC's service to refugees to add and incorporate a parallel service to migrants went up in smoke. However, as I became the first executive of this new enterprise, I discovered that even in its limitations a small secretariat had certain advantages in trying to develop a number of initiatives.

In the middle of my work on migration, our family suffered a terrible tragedy. Our eldest daughter Suzanne, seven years old, was killed by a train at an unguarded railway crossing on her way back from school. It was 9 January 1963. I was in a meeting at the International Labour Office (ILO) when my secretary phoned me with the news and I raced home. Suzanne had permission to go home on her own, but only by taking the guarded crossing. Why she took the other road that morning, we will never know.

The weeks and months following the accident were the saddest time of our life. Had it not been for the ecumenical fellowship we experienced daily, we might not have survived. Visser 't Hooft conducted the funeral service with many people from the WCC present, and Suzanne was laid to rest in the cemetery of Mies, the village where we lived near Geneva. We were surrounded daily by tangible signs of friendship and solidarity from many sides, including meals brought to our house by people who were afraid we would forget to eat. For us, the most important thing was to be as close to our children as possible. Suzanne's three sisters, Inge, Anne Marie, and Emilie, were respectively 6, 4, and 7 months old. Our son Frederik had not yet been born.

Beyond established pastoral and social care

One of my initiatives following the New Delhi assembly was what became our regular publication in several languages, *Migration Today*. Besides reporting what others were doing in this field, I tried to draw special attention to the plight and needs of migrant workers, particularly in Western Europe. Development cooperation was becoming an issue and I sought contributions from qualified people willing to explain how migrant workers – who would sooner or later return to their home country, voluntarily or involuntarily – could become an asset to their societies if properly trained while working abroad. This would be considered a form of development cooperation between the "sending" and "receiving" countries, and governments should develop programmes encouraging migrant workers along these lines. But companies hiring migrant workers were only interested in making profits, while trade unions wanted to protect their own members and governments considered the hiring and training of migrants a matter for the employers.

I made a few speeches in West Germany, Holland, and France but there was relatively little interest in the issue. Once I was invited by the department of social affairs of the government of Hessen-Nassau in Germany to address a conference of social workers. On arrival, I was asked what honorarium I would need for my speech. Was it going to be *ein kleines, mittleres oder ein grosses Referat* (a small, medium or major speech)? I didn't have a clue and said to the official that he should decide after having listened to me. After my speech they decided I had delivered a "major" speech! I was of course delighted to receive an envelope with three or four hundred marks. I decided that I would keep the money, contrary to WCC practice, to pay for a new raincoat: the old one had been stolen at the transfer desk of Miami airport when I was on an official trip for the WCC. I claimed a reimbursement for a new one from the WCC, which was insured for such cases. But Frank Northam, the WCC's treasurer, reacted coolly by arguing that if a female staff member lost her fur coat, she would not be compensated either! On my reply that no WCC female staff member could afford a fur coat on her salary, Northam decided he couldn't win and agreed to the deal!

In Western Europe, Protestant and Roman Catholic churches did not know how to cope with Greek Orthodox migrants, and some Catholic agencies even seemed to see Orthodox workers as potential converts. The Orthodox, on the other hand, appointed bishops in the diaspora, especially in West Germany and with considerable help from the EKD (Evangelical Church in Germany). Muslims depended usually on the policies of their home countries. Their embassies, consulates, and information services kept a close eye on their citizens, creating national associations and building mosques abroad, and even spying on them in some cases.

There were of course exceptions, as, for instance, the hospitality the EKD showed to Orthodox migrants in Germany because of the German churches' long-standing tradition of Orthodox theologians studying in Germany.

The WCC's call to go beyond established pastoral and social care did not meet with much enthusiasm, except for Cimade, the French ecumenical organization, which had a long tradition of caring for refugees and migrants. Jacques Beaumont and his colleagues were open to our initiatives and we held several meetings to try and invent new forms of solidarity. In fact – and this became our second initiative in the Migration secretariat – I wanted to create something similar to the *prêtres ouvriers* (worker priests) in France.

This movement started in order to address the growing gap between the "de-Christianized masses" and the Christian community. Perceiving that young workers entering a "middle-class church" were almost inevitably forced to desert their own milieu, two chaplain-sociologists (Henri Godin and Yvan Daniel) proposed that the

Roman Catholic Church create mission communities in France among the working class. The worker-priest movement was born in the early 1950s when four priests from the Paris Mission asked for permission to seek jobs as a way of getting to know workers and their world. Cardinal Suhard of Paris agreed to their request, but traditional circles swiftly reacted with protests to the Vatican. In 1954 an abrupt order came to a hundred worker-priests to leave their workplaces and return to traditional priestly functions. Most made the painful decision to abandon their jobs, but some felt obliged to continue their mission and broke with the church. They felt betrayed and considered solidarity with their fellow-workers on the factory floor more important. The movement spread to other European countries, notably Italy, Spain, Belgium, and Germany, and in Britain there were some 700 Anglican worker priests.

I had always been impressed by the radical worker-priest model as a way of breaking with the traditional "looking after" and working-for-others concept. It seemed to me that the WCC member churches, when dealing with the integration of migrant workers, needed to encourage the worker-priest experiment as a way of reaching out and being more directly related to the concerns of foreigners. The churches tend to believe that the activity and presence of God are confined within the boundaries of the church, and that "shalom" is to be found only there. But each time someone acts as a true neighbour, each time one lives for others, the life-giving action of God can be discerned. This is the church living for others (Bonhoeffer).[5]

In 1962, during a work camp in Agapè, the ecumenical centre of the Waldensian Church in Italy, I had made contact with what became the Krifteler Group (named after the German village where they lived and worked). They were an ecumenical team of some twelve young people of different nationalities, women and men, who decided to do manual labour alongside migrant workers in the Hoechst Farbwerke AG near Frankfurt-am-Main, as well as in other factories in the same neighbourhood. It was a form of presence and solidarity with workers who came mainly from Italy, Greece, Spain, and Portugal and who knew little or nothing of labour conditions in German industry. The members of the Krifteler Group all became trade unionists.

Two theologians, Holger Samson and Christian Müller, tried to clarify the biblical notion of solidarity in this context. Building bridges with the local churches proved to be difficult: the cultural, political, and social distance between the local German parishioners and the foreign workers was usually too great. The group had contacts with the well-known Italian leftist philosopher and activist Danilo Dolci, who was involved in awareness-building among Sicilians. He came to meet with them and discuss his philosophy and methods: non-violent revolution to change the world by helping people to become aware of their own local and personal problems and find ways to solve them. Equally, Paolo Freire's ideas of awareness-building (conscientization) were used by the team in their relations with the foreign workers on the factory floor.

I soon became an "external" member, together with Giorgio Girardet, one of the initiators of the Krifteler Group and a pastor of the Waldensian Church. I regularly met with them to learn about their experience, life in the factory, the relationship between foreign and German workers, the role of the trade unions, and the reactions of the local churches. Political issues soon surfaced.

For instance, there were serious tensions among Greek migrants about the dictatorial regime of the Greek colonels (1967-74). One of the Krifteler team members, Wim van Es, joined Greeks agitating against that regime on the factory floor. He was later employed by the diaconal section of the EKD as a social worker for Greeks. His activities made him enemies as well as friends among the Greeks. Wim took life according to the gospel very seriously. In 1969 he was murdered in his office by a Greek who was said to be unbalanced. The assassin was tried and sent to prison, but there were suspicions that he had been hired by the Greek intelligence services. Obviously, the murder shocked us all, and the Krifteler team members went through a difficult process of reorientation. But the group has remained for me the symbol of what the churches should be doing: working locally alongside *with*, rather than *for*, foreigners and sharing their conditions and aspirations.

My responsibility vis-à-vis the Krifteler Group was limited to information and interpretation of what was happening in other parts of the world and how the ecumenical movement was relating to or involving itself in conflict situations in Vietnam, Cuba, and Nicaragua. The group was particularly interested in the civil-rights movement in the US, Martin Luther King, and the liberation movements in Southern Africa and in Latin America. Dorothee Sölle in Germany, Danilo Dolci and Tullio Vinay in Riesi, and Giorgio Girardet and Agapè in Italy were some of their main references. They advocated signs of hope expressing a different future, a more just society. They conducted Bible studies on socio-political issues. They did not want publicity and remained anchored to their base among the workers in the factory. All this took place during the 1960s, when we believed that we were living in a period of "exodus" – out of slavery and on the road to the Promised Land!

The Krifteler Group also contributed to discussions at the WCC Arnoldshain conference in 1963, a first regional meeting on migrant workers in Western Europe that I organized and which gathered for the first time some sixty church representatives and trade unionists from both "sending" and "receiving" countries, as well as several migrants.

Just before the conference, Peter Heyde,[6] an economist from Germany delegated by the EKD, and I went to visit the highly respected Ecumenical Patriarch Athenagoras in Constantinople to discuss the needs of Greek Orthodox migrants in Western Europe who were under his jurisdiction. It was an encounter I would not forget. I was deeply impressed by this spiritual leader. He listened carefully to what we had to say and showed great concern for people on the move who were in danger of losing their identity and faith. We received his strong support for finding solutions and he expressed his gratitude for the work the WCC was doing in this field.

In my opening remarks at Arnoldshain I emphasized that migrant workers were at best tolerated and often seen as a necessary evil. But shouldn't we as Christians consider the issue from a different angle: Shouldn't the free movement of workers be seen rather as a prelude to the coming pluralistic society of an integrated Europe? And shouldn't this migration lead us to rethink our concept of this future society?

Migrant workers are another opportunity for the churches to reconsider the original meaning of the local congregation.

André Philip, a sharp-minded former French socialist government minister, political economist, and committed Christian, chaired the preparatory committee and the meeting itself. He spoke of the need for protection of migrants, as well as their integration into the social and economic life of the receiving countries. New intra-European legislation in the field was required urgently. Like us, he was convinced of the need for a European secretariat to deal with the matter, and in fact discussions led to what I had been hoping for: the creation of the Churches' Commission for Migrants in Europe (CCME), temporarily attached to the WCC migration secretariat, with me as secretary of both.[7] Not long afterwards, my long-time and committed colleague in the migration secretariat, Chantal Scheidecker, took over as secretary of the committee.

Looking back now, I realize that the creation of this committee on West European migration proved to be a significant ecumenical initiative. Later, the committee moved to Brussels to be closer to the European Union (EU). It cooperates with CEC and plays its role in representing member churches at the EU while keeping them informed about the development of European policies in this field. In fact, it plays an essential role by constantly confronting the EU with the realities of the lives of migrants and challenging it to take appropriate action.

4. Uppsala, 1968

One of the main issues encountered during my period in the migration secretariat was discrimination and racism. The WCC had been concerned about race relations from its inception in 1948, but it took until 1959 before the council appointed Dai Kitagawa as the first executive of the secretariat on race and ethnic relations. His US/Japanese background – he had been interned by the Americans in the US after the Japanese attack on Pearl Harbor in 1941 – made him very suitable for the job. And besides, he was a confidence-inspiring person who would spend weeks or months in difficult ethnic/race situations – such as Ceylon, where I witnessed his capabilities in 1961 when he listened carefully to both Singhalese and Tamils and tried to mediate between them. Mediation was his great gift.

However, as we were preparing for the WCC's 4th assembly in Uppsala in 1968, it was clear that statements and goodwill missions were no longer enough. They didn't have the desired effect. Eugene Carson Blake, as the chief executive of the Presbyterian Church in the

USA –who had succeeded Visser 't Hooft as general secretary of the World Council in 1966 – had been deeply involved in the civil-rights struggle in his own country. From his experience, he was well aware that the WCC had to move from statements to action.

But there was another even more pressing reason: apartheid in South Africa was moving the country to the brink of civil war and the churches there were very much part of the problem. Consultations in the 1960s – notably at Cottesloe, South Africa (1961), and Mindolo, Zambia (1964) – had not resulted in any tangible change. On the contrary, the white South African government was constantly reinforcing its racist policies with the blessing and support of most of the white church leadership. Moreover, in Southern Africa several countries still under colonial rule were struggling for independence. Liberation movements in Mozambique, Angola, Guinea-Bissão, Rhodesia/Zimbabwe, and Namibia demanded recognition and support.

A major contribution to the debate on racism was made by the WCC's pivotal 1966 world conference on "Church and Society," which was probably the first with full representation from the "third world" as well as a large group of Roman Catholic observers. It closely followed the convening of Vatican II by Pope John XXIII, which catapulted the Roman Catholic Church into full ecumenical involvement. The 1960s was a time of astonishingly rapid transition. In many respects it laid the foundation for the development of liberation theology. The Church and Society conference stood in the spirit and tradition of the 1925 Stockholm "Life and Work" conference and the 1937 Oxford conference on "Church, Community and State." In fact, the 1966 conference would later be considered as the third world conference on church and society.

One of the speakers was Eduardo Mondlane, the leader of the Mozambican liberation movement Frelimo, who emphasized the need for non-Western peoples to have recourse to self-help in the absence of any willingness on the part of the colonial powers to give up their power.

Martin Luther King had accepted to preach at the Sunday morning service in Geneva's St Pierre cathedral, but he had to cancel his presence at the last minute because of the Chicago race riots. His sermon was to have been broadcast on the Eurovision network and his cancellation caused considerable confusion. In the end, the sermon was filmed in Chicago and brought to Geneva in time for it to be presented from the pulpit of St Pierre. It made a deep impression on us all.

I was one of the conference secretaries, and together with Dai Kitagawa we helped draft reports on discrimination and racism. One particular event was the march of conference participants from the Ecumenical Centre to the Palais des Nations to demonstrate to the UN the Christian concern for world peace and social justice. Visser 't Hooft and others had originally opposed the march, but the youth participants received support and in the end the march took place, with many others joining in. About 350 marchers went to the entrance of the Palais des Nations and made their strong affirmation of peace and justice in solidarity with the principles of the UN. What struck me most in the reports was one sentence in the text on the rights of minorities and of oppressed groups, which stated that Christians had to give special attention to the defence of those who "do not have access to power and cannot effectively exercise or defend their rights."[1]

The 1966 conference prepared the way for certain key decisions that were made at the WCC's assembly in Uppsala in 1968, notably on racism and development and gender issues. Foremost, the conference stressed the need for solidarity with movements of the victims of current socio-political crises. It confronted participants with existing realities, stating,

> Revolutionary thought and action, the basic rejection of the present world system of power and order and the determination to overthrow it, are more alive in our world than in that of a generation ago. This revolutionary stance may arise within a nation, a racial group, a class or a generation.[2]

Racism emerges as a major issue

Many churches from the so-called developing world had joined WCC in the 1960s after political independence. From their perspective, racism was a major issue that needed to be addressed in a new way. At the time of its foundation in 1948, the WCC counted among its 146 member churches only 42 from the third world (including ten African churches from South Africa, Egypt, and Ethiopia). By the time of the Uppsala assembly, their number had increased to 103 out of 253. Of the 41 African churches, the majority were now from independent Africa. The WCC had more truly become a world council.

In this context, the issue of racism was being taken up with new energy by those who were its victims. The suffering notably of the black people in Southern Africa and the US deeply affected the ecumenical movement. It was therefore only natural that Martin Luther King should be invited to be the opening preacher at Uppsala. By linking racism with poverty and oppression, and speaking up about the war in Vietnam, King had opened our eyes to situations the world over. And not only that, his biblical message of non-violence to achieve basic change made us feel that he was a prophet for our times. Here was someone we could trust. He was a true servant of God.

King's assassination shortly before the assembly only underscored the importance of the issue. The silencing of this prophetic voice stunned the world. For us in the WCC, who had heard his voice time and again, it was a terrible blow to our morale and faith in a better world. We had lost a "rassembleur" of people far beyond the churches, a man who inspired confidence, even though or precisely because he was preaching the difficult message of conversion. What remained after his death was his challenge and cry, "I have a dream" (1963 March on Washington). It made us more determined to continue what he and others had started. And at the same time it is what we continue to say to each other when we want to make it clear that we have not lost hope in a more just world.

A few months before Uppsala, Blake asked three WCC staff members – Rena Karefa Smart (an African American), David Gill (white from Australia), and me – to examine the assembly programme with a view to identifying where and how the issue of racism could helpfully be introduced. We met regularly and reported directly to Blake. During the assembly, an ad-hoc group of some ten delegates and staff met daily at breakfast time or in a corner of the assembly hall and worked on a statement on racism in all parts in the world and on white racism in particular. Each of us participated in different sections and committees of the assembly, seeking to ensure adequate discussion of the issue. We would review progress and find the right people to introduce the issue in the day's sessions. There was good cooperation on all sides, though sometimes we had to push hard. Thus, we were a kind of lobby. Rena Karefa Smart especially proved to have an impressive power to convince people of the importance of the issue. As a black person, she worked intelligently and also emotionally on the conscience of her white colleagues and assembly delegates to accept their responsibility for the past, be it slavery or colonial rule.

My own thoughts were, and still are, quite clear. I find it hard to accept that I am responsible for what past generations have done. Do I have to identify with the slave-traders or my colonial ancestors? Should the culprits of racism in the past still burden me with their crimes today? Or am I responsible only for my own acts and those of my own generation? Our Dutch history tells us clearly about our colonialist behaviour in the Dutch East Indies and our contribution to the apartheid policies in South Africa ever since Jan van Riebeek landed in the Cape in 1652.

I am reminded of my maternal great-great-grandfather, Frederiks' Jacob, who, as already mentioned, had been governor-general of the Dutch East Indies (1881-84). He no doubt carried out the harsh colonial policies of his government in The Hague. Earlier, he had been a successful producer and trader of sugar in the Indies and he probably knew how to exploit the Indonesian people in his service. For centuries it was a tradition for enterprising young people to prove themselves by starting their career in the East Indies. There was enormous Dutch investment there, and the Netherlands became a rich country through its colonial policies and by exploiting millions of indigenous people.

I cannot ignore what we now consider the inhuman behaviour of our fore-fathers and mothers. Even if we are not directly responsible for what they did in the past, I believe there is collective responsibility for what happened. However, the crucial question now is whether we have learned from history and are ready to take an active part in combating racism *today*. Our answers to those questions will have a bearing on the generation of my children and grandchildren as they are confronted by these and similar issues in their own context.

James Baldwin: Catalyst for action

In last-minute preparations for the assembly, Blake and we as staff had come to the conclusion that there was simply no adequate replacement possible for King as the preacher at the opening session of the assembly. In the end, the well-known black American author James Baldwin was invited, but only after lengthy discussions. There was criticism of the choice of this son of a Baptist minister: for one, he was known to be a homosexual and not a church-related person. The compromise was to have him speak in the evening programme at the university and not in the main assembly hall.

When Baldwin finally spoke, it was immediately clear that he had been the right choice. In a vibrant address on the theme "White Racism or World Community?" he introduced himself as "one of God's creatures whom the Christian church has most betrayed." Recapitulating the long story of racial injustice, he charged that

> long ago, for a complex of reasons, but among them power, the Christian personality split itself into two – into dark and light, and is now bewildered and at war with itself ... I wonder if there is left in the Christian civilizations the moral energy, the spiritual daring, to atone, to repent, to be born again?[3]

Baldwin electrified his audience, and afterwards we all felt that he had found the right tone and helped to make the assembly move from words to action. He made a lasting impression on me personally, and it propelled me into taking on the responsibilities that lay ahead.

The Uppsala assembly became a landmark. Twenty years after its foundation, the WCC had accepted that a new type of response was needed to the most urgent challenges of our world. It was the time of liberation theologians, particularly in Latin and North America. It was also a time of crisis, protest, and resistance against existing social and political structures, against the war in Vietnam, and in support of the liberation movement in the Portuguese colonies in Southern Africa as well as in Rhodesia, Namibia, and South Africa.

The ecumenical fellowship clearly recognized in these developments a *kairos*, a God-given opportunity. Racism was not just one among many injustices: it was a specific Christian heresy. Thus there was a special challenge to pass from words to acts of solidarity with the racially oppressed. A sense of urgency was emerging. The much-needed theological, ethical, and ecclesiological debate about the implications of a programme of action would have to take place along the road of implementation, after first taking risks.

For me personally, Uppsala was an experience I would never forget. I had participated in the New Delhi assembly. The difference between the two was enormous! Delhi was solemn. It was the time when the International Missionary Council (IMC) and the Russian and other Eastern Orthodox churches formally joined WCC, and dialogue between the churches of the Eastern and the Western tradition gained importance after a separation of more than a thousand years. The entry of the Russian Orthodox bishops in a long, exclusively male (and bearded) ceremonial procession in dark robes was intimidating! We were yet to discover what lay under those robes and beards!

The connection between power and racism

Racism was not the only major issue that surfaced at the Uppsala assembly. Some participants asked for a clear link to be made between the elimination of racism and a redistribution of power. In his dramatic keynote speech, Kenneth Kaunda, first president of an independent Zambia (1965), spoke of the poor and rich countries and the need to share power. Development and racism had in common the issue of the powerful and powerless. These mutually reinforced the question of the need for a redistribution of power, not only between nations but also between churches.

This upset more than one church leader. Some of the West German bishops especially objected to such revolutionary proposals as, for example, the redistribution of power. Elisabeth Adler from East Germany, responding to Visser 't Hooft's speech on the mandate of the ecumenical movement, spoke out very firmly, asking whether ecumenism could ever become officially part of the established churches. She was critical of his intervention and feared a loss of the movement's dynamism to renew church and society. She made a case for non-ecclesiastical ecumenism, or even a post-ecumenical movement of Christian renewal. Ecumenism should not be equated with the Establishment! This was a new element in the discussion and it appealed to many of us. Criticism of one of the founding fathers of the ecumenical movement had been unheard of! It then dawned on me that a younger generation in the ecumenical movement was in the process of taking over from the pioneers who had been unable to face worldwide racism in the churches. But even we were still dreaming that we could eliminate racism in a few years.

Finally, the assembly made clear analyses and recommendations, particularly on racism. We were no longer exclusively concerned about personal attitudes. We perceived that structural and collective racism through power mechanisms and economic systems were much more dangerous. Churches, governments, and multinational corporations exploiting their employees needed to be challenged. Above all, the churches themselves had to take bold decisions to eliminate racism within their ranks before they could, in all genuineness, take part in the wider struggle in society. Uppsala, for the first time in WCC history, called racism and white racism in particular "a blatant denial of the Christian faith."[4] No single assembly section had been given the task of dealing specifically with the race issue; it was taken up by five of the six sections, including those on the catholicity of the church and on worship.

Our ad-hoc group had finalized a draft statement on white racism and Blake agreed that it should be distributed to the assembly delegates. But to our surprise and anger, it was not discussed; instead it was referred to the newly elected central committee. The paper included definitions of racism and white racism, an analysis of areas of particular racial crisis, and a discussion of the challenge that racism presents to Christians, the churches, and Christian theology. In spite of its unofficial character, it became the basis for the crash programme recommended in the report of the committee on Church and Society to be launched by the WCC itself in order to show the way for the member churches. Central to all this was that combating racism was a matter of Christian social and political responsibility, and above all a matter of the integrity of our faith.

There was a tremendous will to move from words to action. The example of Martin Luther King and the need to continue his work influenced us profoundly. By a standing vote, the assembly expressed its deep sense of the loss to the church caused by his assassination and recommended that the WCC undertake a study of non-violent methods for achieving social change (Martin Luther King resolution).[5]

The inspiration of liberation leaders

Uppsala was probably my most exciting ecumenical meeting ever. It had a far greater influence on me than any previous or later gathering. We believed – naively – that the exodus to the Promised Land had started, that we were part of that exodus from the land of slavery and on the road to liberation from oppression, toward a world not simply without war but of justice and real peace.

We knew of course that we had a hard struggle ahead of us, but we were convinced that this new world was within reach. It demanded total commitment from us. And we were ready to take the risks involved. Uppsala became part of the general mood of optimism of the 1960s and especially of the year 1968, with all its rebellion and revolt. Following the decolonization process and the process of liberation in Asia and Africa, there was need for renewal of the West. The churches needed to change and be confronted with the new social and political realities.

Were we over-reaching ourselves in our expectations as to what we were capable of? Certainly! But it gave us the strength to plan and to move ahead. The example of liberation movement leaders inspired us: especially Eduardo Mondlane from Mozambique, whom I had heard at the 1966 Church and Society conference; Agostinho Neto from Angola (a medical doctor – about the only one in Angola – who died in 1979); Amilcar Cabral, whom I met in Rome at a conference and who was killed in 1973; Herbert Chitepo of Zimbabwe (killed in 1975); and last but not least Nelson Mandela and Oliver (OR, as his close friends called him) Tambo, who during my time with the Programme to Combat Racism became a personal friend and with whom I developed a privileged relationship when he was leading the African National Congress (ANC) in exile as acting president during the time of Mandela's imprisonment on Robben Island. (It was a very special honour and moving experience for me to receive in 2004 in Pretoria – ten years after the first democratic elections in South Africa – from the hands of President Thabo Mbeki the award of Grand Companion of the Order of OR Tambo.) Tambo died in 1993, just before the liberation of South Africa. He came to see us regularly in Geneva to brief us about the situation there and particularly about the problems of the ANC in its struggle against the apartheid regime. I also visited him in his different "hide-outs" and ANC field offices or at his temporary home in London, where his wife Adelaide was working as a nurse.

All these leaders were, in the best sense of the word the "products of Christian mission," Protestant or Roman Catholic. They had been at Christian boarding schools, and both Tambo and Mandela had studied at Fort Hare University in South Africa, which had grown out of a (Presbyterian) Church of Scotland mission-run secondary school. Fort Hare – where Z. K. Matthews, a former president of the ANC and later secretary for Africa in the WCC, had been teaching – was then the only institution of higher learning open to African students. Tambo studied law and later associated himself with Nelson Mandela to open the first black law practice in Johannesburg.

On the way back home from Uppsala, I wondered how I could share this extraordinary experience with my wife and my family in Holland. Trying to make them understand everything that had happened and how we could go forward was going to be difficult. But if I could not involve them in what was for us a true conversion, was there any credibility at all in what we were trying to do? If I didn't succeed in explaining and convincing those nearest to me of what I was experiencing and the transformation I was going through, then what chances were there of communicating our convictions and converting the churches? This was going to be a test! It was time to break with the past.

5. Notting Hill and Canterbury, 1969

The next station on my journey was to be Notting Hill, London. After the Uppsala assembly, Gene Blake soon decided that the existing "triumvirate" of Rena Karefa Smart, David Gill, and me were to prepare the consultation that had been decided by the new central committee to work on concrete proposals to the WCC and its member churches on how to fight racism in the period ahead. We collected names of potential participants, identified issues that needed priority attention at the meeting, and solicited preparatory papers and reports. We decided that the Methodist centre at Notting Hill, London (an area of racial tension), was to be the venue. In January 1969 I flew to Dar es Salaam (Tanzania) to meet Eduardo Mondlane and invite him to be the keynote speaker at the consultation. Mondlane was the president of Frelimo, the liberation movement of Mozambique, which was still

49

a Portuguese colony. He had established his headquarters in Dar es Salaam, invited by the Tanzanian government and in particular by its president, Julius Nyerere.

Nicolas Maro, general secretary of the Christian Council of Tanzania, had arranged the meeting with Mondlane, but the Frelimo president was extremely busy, in and out of already liberated territory in Mozambique, inspecting Frelimo guerrilla fighters, as well as visiting friendly countries to drum up support for the movement. I had to wait several days to see him, which gave me the opportunity to visit the Mozambican Institute in Dar, run by Mondlane's (American) wife, Janet. The institute was a secondary school for some 120 Mozambican refugee children. It also arranged for scholarships to foreign institutes of higher studies for those refugees who possessed suitable qualifications.

The liberation of Mozambique was not only a matter of driving out the Portuguese regime. It also meant constructing a new, independent society without hunger and without discrimination, as well as dealing with tribalism and traditional chiefdoms, which the Portuguese played off against each other. Frelimo became socialist- and Marxist-oriented once it turned out that Western countries were unwilling to support a movement that fought a war against colonial Portugal, an ally and a member of NATO.

Finally, on 30 January 1969, Mondlane confirmed our appointment, and Maro and I went to his headquarters in a villa on the outskirts of Dar. There a guard told us Eduardo was still in a meeting and we were asked to proceed to the nearby Oyster Bay Hotel where he would join us. When he arrived, I was amazed to see him all by himself – no security guards in sight! A very tall man, he climbed out of a small rented Ford Anglia with some difficulty. While sipping our afternoon tea, I made my request for him to be the keynote speaker at the public meeting we were organizing at Church House, Westminster, London, as part of the Notting Hill consultation. We wanted him to explain to a large, mostly Western and not exclusively church audience why he and his movement had decided to use arms against the Portuguese in order to liberate themselves. How had they come to this decision and what did this mean to him as a committed

Christian? What exactly did they want to achieve? And what did they expect, in their struggle, from the churches outside Mozambique and from the ecumenical movement?

Mondlane was familiar with WCC thinking, as he had been a youth participant at the council's 1954 assembly in Evanston, and a speaker at the 1966 Church and Society conference in Geneva as well as at the 1964 WCC Mindolo ecumenical consultation on race in Kitwe, Zambia, held in cooperation with the All Africa Conference of Churches (AACC) and the South African Institute of Race Relations. The latter meeting had been organized by Daisuke Kitagawa (in charge of the WCC secretariat on race and ethnic relations) and chaired by Z. K. Matthews. It was at Mindolo that Mondlane explained how Frelimo had decided to take up arms in violent resistance against the Portuguese colonial rulers. He explained, too, the moral and spiritual problems of the armed struggle with which he was now confronted. We wanted him to speak out at the London meeting about these issues and so to confront the churches and public opinion with a situation they largely preferred to ignore.

Mondlane accepted the invitation without hesitation. Before leaving I couldn't resist asking him why he had no guards to protect him in a place full of tourists like the hotel. He shrugged his shoulders and laughed – he didn't seem to be concerned in the least.

I was of course delighted with the result of our conversation and left the next morning for Nairobi on my way back to Geneva. It was there that I heard on the BBC the terrible news that Mondlane had been assassinated by a parcel bomb three days after our meeting, on 3 February 1969. I couldn't believe it – I felt paralyzed. Then I remembered our conversation about his security. In a stroke, we had lost one of the most promising third-world leaders, someone who would no doubt have been a formidable first president of an independent Mozambique.

Mondlane: A person of faith

I came to know Mondlane (1920-69) first during the Church and Society conference. He had received a PhD from Northwestern University in Chicago, US, and held a prominent UN position before deciding to give his full energy to the liberation of his people. What he said at Mindolo reflected a new reality: the conflict between the colonized peoples of Southern Africa and their Portuguese oppressors had deepened; peaceful solutions were becoming increasingly difficult to find. In this context, participants were reminded by Visser 't Hooft that in certain situations of oppression, one of the "good works" of Christians could be to eliminate the tyrant. This had been the case in Germany during the Second World War when Dietrich Bonhoeffer had decided there was no alternative but to try and eliminate Hitler. Armed resistance could therefore not be ruled out.

Mondlane was closely associated with the (Reformed) Swiss Mission from his early years. But as time went on, he came to believe that his involvement in achieving independence for his country needed to be broader than his participation in the life and work of the church. By the end of his life he found himself alienated from many people in the church, principally because of his decision to be engaged in armed struggle. Nevertheless, he understood himself to be a person of faith, and he pushed the churches to engage with the world around them and to respond to the call for justice in the face of colonial oppression. He challenged the churches and missions to break with colonialism and racism because of the clear call of the Gospel.[1]

Mondlane also raised the issue at the Church and Society conference and would no doubt have reinforced his challenge as keynote speaker at the Notting Hill consultation. He had experienced racism not only in his own country but particularly in the churches and missions in South Africa, where he studied at a school of social work in Johannesburg and at Wits University in the 1940s. He was involved in the ANC youth league until he was expelled from the country in 1949. In that same year he was detained and interrogated by the Portuguese secret service, before being released. The object was clearly to scare him and to discourage him from his activities against the colonial regime.

In 1951 he went to study sociology at Oberlin College, Ohio, in the US. In 1960 he met and later married the white American student, Janet Johnson (she joined him in the struggle for liberation by founding the Mozambican Institute in Dar es Salaam). At the Evanston assembly in 1954, Mondlane was a youth consultant representing the Swiss Mission in Portuguese East Africa, the only representative of Mozambique at the meeting. This worldwide ecumenical gathering greatly impressed him and he immediately saw its significance for furthering the independence of Mozambique. It could be claimed that Mondlane was one of the key voices that finally led the WCC to set up the Programme to Combat Racism (PCR).

Tambo: "The gospel is about liberation"

When I got back to Geneva, we discussed possibilities for replacing Mondlane and agreed to invite Oliver Tambo (1917-93), the acting president of the African National Congress (ANC). Tambo spent much of his time in London. He was sensitive to our invitation as he had been briefed, at our request, by Archbishop Trevor Huddleston. We decided that both of them should be keynote speakers at the planned public meeting in Church House, Westminster.

During the Notting Hill consultation, 19-24 May 1969, we were confronted twice with unexpected incidents. The first came during the public meeting, in Church House. A group of right-wing extremists from the National Front hurled abuse at Archbishop Huddleston and later screamed their white racist slogans at Oliver Tambo. The police had to intervene so that the speakers could continue. The incident shocked and shamed us all.

One particular moment during my PCR years that I will never forget was when Tambo came to see me in my office in 1975. He asked me how I was doing. It was a time when I was depressed about the attitudes of certain churches in the West with regard to our involvement in Southern Africa. So I answered that I was not happy. He asked why and I explained. His answer unexpectedly revealed his faith. He said, "Where I was brought up, in an Anglican boarding school in South Africa, we were read the scripture lesson every day. And the one thing that I have understood from the Bible during those years is that the gospel is about liberation; liberation not just of me personally but liberation also of my people. That is what I am involved in day after day. That is what the liberation movement is about. Can't you tell this to your German bishops?"

I was stunned. Never had I heard such a clear message from any church leader. So I asked him whether he would join me and address a meeting of church leaders and testify to his faith. But Tambo looked at me with a twinkle in his eye and said, "Brother, I have my responsibilities of keeping my movement together, and you have your responsibilities vis-à-vis your member churches. But if you want you can quote me." From that moment on I knew Tambo and I had a lasting relationship. Only later did I learn that he was a devout Christian and that he had once considered a vocation in the priesthood of the Anglican church.

We met several times at his home in Muswell Hill, North London, but also in his offices in Zambia and in hotels somewhere in between. He shared with me his worries, and his despair after the Pretoria regime had succeeded in squeezing the ANC out of Mozambique as a result of the Nkomati accord in 1984, which compelled both parties (South Africa, but of course particularly Mozambique) to cease helping each other's enemies. These became the darkest days for the ANC and for its leader in particular. I met OR, as his friends were allowed to call him, shortly afterwards in Lusaka in a place away from his office and saw before me a lonely and sombre man. He felt betrayed by his friend Samora Machel (then president of Mozambique), who had not warned him of the accord and who was trying to portray it as a victory for his country. "How shall we interpret this to our people?" said OR, looking into the distance. "I will have to explain to my people how this accord will affect us." Mozambique's willingness to let the ANC operate from its territory had been a major step forward in its liberation struggle. Now that it was forced out as a result of Pretoria's insistence, the ANC's strategy was up in the air and Tambo was only too aware of the possible consequences. Also, Mozambique had been weakened and become Pretoria's servant. This was a disastrous situation. The ANC had to reconsider its long-term policy.

I realized that Tambo had allowed me to witness his extreme loneliness at that moment. He was the only person who could hold the ANC together, both overseas and internally, in the face of the innumerable challenges from the apartheid regime and Western indifference. The following years would show his extraordinary and brave leadership.

He did not live to see the full fruits of his labour. In 1990, following a stroke, he attended the ANC conference in Johannesburg. He chose to become chairman of the ANC instead of president, a position that Nelson Mandela assumed after his release from prison. He died in April 1993, one year before the first democratic elections in South Africa, and was buried in Wattville, Benoni, South Africa. He was a small but great man. I am proud that the distinction I received from the government of South Africa in 2004 carries his name.

A serious challenge to "white double-dealing"

The second interruption at the Notting Hill meeting took place during the final evening session, while we were discussing the reports of the working groups. A small group of young black people suddenly entered our meeting room and politely took over the microphone. Their leader, who later gave his name as George Black, read a "Declaration of Revolution," which began,

> For hundreds of years, white Christians have taught black people to love their neighbours; to be meek, humble and obedient; to love their white God; above all – to be non-violent, to turn the other cheek. But this is only one other instance of white double-standard,

of white double-dealing. To the white man Christianity has taught only *power* – with military, economic and political power ... Today, we say that ... meekness in the face of exploitation is a crime ... What is good for the white Christian is good for the non-white. We are saying that when a white Christian strikes a non-white, the non-white should pick up his gun. We are tired of a religion in which the greatest black Christians are martyrs and saints, the greatest white Christians the imperialist *conquistadores* and administrators who put them to death. Instead of "Onward Christian Soldiers," we are saying "Onward Freedom Fighters" ... Instead of red power, black power, brown power and yellow power to white Christians, we are saying black power to black people, brown power to brown people, yellow power to yellow people, and red power to red people. And this means political, economic and military power.[2]

And quoting Malcolm X, he concluded, "Political power grows out of the barrel of a gun. Anyone who desires freedom must be willing to die for it."

The declaration demanded, among other things, £5 million for a defence fund for certain named political prisoners and £30 million for liberation movements in Vietnam, Angola, Mozambique, Portuguese Guinea, and Rhodesia. It also demanded "the publication of the assets, holdings, investments (direct or in portfolio) and financial operations of all member organizations of the World Council of Churches." The group promised to return the next morning to receive a legal document acceding to its demands.

The result of this unpleasant visit was that the consultation spent until late in the night as well as the next morning debating these demands. Arguments of support for the demands came mainly from some of the black participants, involved in the black revolution in the US. They underlined that the churches were part of the problem and identified with the status quo. Others said that as Christians we should express more forcefully our guilt, past and present. But most felt that we should not give in to a set of private demands by anonymous intruders. In fact, the meeting had already debated many of the issues raised by the black group, notably the question of reparations and redistribution of power.

But Gene Blake wanted a clear answer to the black group and at midnight he told Rena Karefa-Smart, David Gill, and me to prepare a draft reply for him to consider at breakfast the next morning. So the three of us divided up our task and went to our rooms, where most of the night we sweated over writing up what we thought the consultation's reply should be. Fortunately, Gene accepted most of it and by 11 A.M. – only an hour before adjournment! – the participants adopted the paper. Ironically, the intruders never showed up to hear our answer, and so Blake read the carefully worded statement to the meeting, making clear that we were not a decision-making body and thus could not accede to the group's demands.

Never in my life had I been exposed to such a tense situation. As a white person I felt mentally and even physically threatened by the presence of some black American activists. Obviously it was part of their strategy to make us feel uncomfortable. Also, it was clear to me that the hard-line American black strategy against whites was not shared by most of the African (and Asian) participants, who had a more subtle way of making their impact felt. The problem for whites was that they could not show any preference for one or the other approach, otherwise they were in danger of alienating themselves from all blacks and thereby putting themselves even more on the defensive. So we had to find our own way, and admit in all honesty our racist tendencies as part of our culture and history, traditions, and beliefs of superiority in past and present. At the same time, we needed to show our readiness to involve ourselves in radical change in church and society, in spite of the cynical reactions we would receive from some blacks.

The WCC executive and central committees take the leap

Blake presented the Notting Hill meeting report and recommendations and the staff document to the executive committee a few months later at Canterbury, UK. There followed a heated debate.

The executive disagreed with the proposed "philosophy" of a pro-gramme to combat racism, particularly with the emphasis on white racism and the suggestion that money should be used from WCC reserves for "reparations" to oppressed racial groups. The opinion of the executive was strengthened by the fact that apparently several members of staff had confidentially reported to the chairman, M. M. Thomas, that there was disagreement within the staff about setting up a new secretariat on racism and about the ideology expressed in the report of the Notting Hill consultation. Also, Asian members of the executive, in particular General Simatupang (Indonesia) and D. T. Niles (Ceylon), argued that the emphasis on racism was exagger-ated and that the particular experience of the civil-rights movement in the US should not be globalized. According to them, the crucial issue to be tackled was the struggle against mass poverty. And in addi-tion, Visser 't Hooft told Thomas that he was critical of the propos-als, which he saw as an extension of American concerns. He was also concerned that the staff document was not sufficiently geared to the Europeans.

M. Thomas maintained that racism and poverty should be major concerns of the ecumenical movement, but he did not agree with all the arguments put forward in the staff document. He suggested that the executive should amend the document before sending it forward to the central committee. Pauline Webb, who had participated in the Notting Hill meeting, urged that the report, based on the recom-mendations of the consultation, go forward unamended to the cen-tral committee, where it could be discussed in a more global context. Her proposal was defeated: 11 were in favour of amending the report before presenting it to the central committee, while 7 voted against.

A sub-committee was appointed, under the chairmanship of Simatupang, to draft a statement that was then presented to the cen-tral committee, despite objection from both Blake and Webb. There followed a long and passionate discussion – I have personally never witnessed such a heated debate in a WCC committee. Members from the third world recalled how colonialism was often based on racist assumptions and how the Christian missions had sometimes played a very dubious role. In particular, Father Paul Verghese of the Syrian

Orthodox Church of the East made a strong plea for a more radical programme. He personally attacked Archbishop Frank Woods of the Anglican Church in Australia for what he said were his white racist attitudes. There was also a debate about the title of the proposed programme. Some members, mostly European, felt that the term "combating" was too radical and not in line with the Christian tradition. Also, there was considerable opposition by the finance committee to the proposed use of WCC reserve funds for the creation of a Special Fund to Combat Racism. It was felt that this was not only financially questionable but also morally wrong.

In the end, the amendments proposed by the executive committee to the original report were defeated and the launch of the Programme to Combat Racism and its Special Fund was adopted, almost unchanged.[3] Blake's leadership had prevailed, and Webb had courageously defended the results of the Notting Hill consultation with success.

It was a truly great moment, for which many of us in the staff had been longing. Previously, the WCC had operated a secretariat on racial and ethnic relations as a result of a recommendation by the Evanston assembly.[4] But it took until 1959 for a secretary (Daisuke Kitagawa) to be appointed, and his mandate was too limited. For the first time in its history, the WCC had a mandate to develop a programme of action on racism and to lead and support its member churches in assuming their responsibilities.

6. From Consultation to Confrontation: The 1970s

Soon after the Canterbury meeting, Blake informed me that in his consultation with staff, my name had been put forward as the director of the new Programme to Combat Racism (PCR). Would I accept? He gave me a couple of days to reflect.

This was a tremendous challenge. My first reaction was astonishment that they would not appoint a "heavyweight" for such an exposed position. I also felt that I would not be up to meeting the tremendous expectations created since the Uppsala assembly. And I was surprised they would choose a white person to head the programme. I was later told that Andrew (Andy) Young, close friend and collaborator of Martin Luther King, had also been on the list of candidates but that he had declined the post, arguing that his priority was to continue in the civil-rights movement, especially after King's assassination. I was also gratified that the WCC seemed ready to invite a lay person to take on the job.

In a letter to the WCC executive committee, Blake wrote,

> After considerable discussion both with staff and constituency, it has been generally agreed that it would be wise, on the staff of three, to have a continental European as the director of this programme, in which case the other two members of the staff should probably be a black American and an Asian or African ..., then the chairman of the international advisory committee should be

the most distinguished African we can find. With the above as the background of our thinking, the officers intend, unless they receive strong objections from many of you, to propose Mr Baldwin Sjollema as the director of the programme. He would have strong staff support for this increase and shift of responsibilities in the World Council staff ... Between now and January 1, Mr Sjollema and the general secretary would be working together seeking other staff members and on the composition of the international advisory committee.[1]

I consulted a few of my friends on the staff about my nomination and was surprised at the support. Albert van den Heuvel (director of Communication) commented, "Your appointment will earn you a few stomach ulcers!" And he was right.

Eugene Blake

Gene Blake's election as general secretary in 1966 had been on the understanding that he was chosen to bridge an interim period. And he considered his mandate as such. But very soon after taking over from Visser 't Hooft, he decided that certain matters needed urgent attention.

One particular issue was that of staff salaries, which Visser 't Hooft had never touched, leaving those matters in the hands of his treasurer, Frank Northam. The result was that we were paid poorly, which caused serious problems especially for families with children. Within a couple of months, Blake made a complete overhaul of the salary system, from which nearly everybody benefited. He was an American church leader and church politician and he combined these talents with good business insights! He was also an excellent organizer. Unfortunately, he never bothered to learn German, even though the German churches were the major financial contributors to most WCC budgets.

One of Blake's characteristics was frankness and directness. After my first meeting of the staff executive group (SEG), which he created in order to make the staff decision-making process easier and more transparent, he said, "Baldwin, I didn't hear you this morning." "No," was my reply. "I was taught to listen when you attend a meeting for the first time." "Well," he replied, "that may be so, but I expect a substantial contribution from you next time SEG meets." So I understood I was not hired to keep my mouth shut!

My sabbatical in 1967 to finish my sociology studies proved to be of enormous help. I remembered my discussion with Blake who, initially, was reluctant to give me study leave but then accepted my reasoning that I would be more useful to the WCC afterwards. He had tested me, and he gave me an extraordinary chance to prove my capacities in the Programme to Combat Racism.

Blake was without doubt the prime mover in the creation of the PCR, even though some alleged that he was importing an "American virus" into the WCC. But his vision was much wider: he was concerned that racism still prevailed in the churches and in society in spite of their teachings over the years. This state of affairs could only be changed if and when the ecumenical movement worldwide became the front-runner in combating it. There was good reason for his special concern about the issue of racism: Blake, who at that time was the stated clerk of the Presbyterian Church USA, had been very close to Martin Luther King and had taken part in the historic 1963 march to Washington. He had been deeply involved in the civil-rights movement and was one of the speakers who preceded King on the podium in Washington. He confessed that despite the US churches' many high-minded resolutions,

> we have achieved neither a desegregated church nor a desegregated society. And it is partly because the churches of America have failed to put their own house in order that one hundred years after the emancipation proclamation ... the United States of America still faces a racial crisis.[2]

He once stated that "the ecumenical movement is a result of concerns of ordinary people who find their ecumenical aspirations limited to church structures." Though I don't accept the latter part of his statement, I do agree that the ecumenical movement will only advance if and when "ordinary Christians" believe in it and make it their priority. Blake, much more than his predecessor Visser 't Hooft, understood that the ecumenical movement is not merely a gathering of pioneers and church leaders, but a movement that has to grow from below.

The immediate question was: Who would be my closest supporters among my WCC colleagues? Soon it became clear to me that I needed to turn especially to Philip Potter, from the small Caribbean island of Dominica, who as director of the division on world mission and evangelism played an important role in the life of the WCC. I felt I could expect most help from him. Strangely enough, Blake did not directly involve Potter in the process that led to the creation of the PCR. He was not at the Notting Hill consultation. Yet with Potter I could share my concerns. And I had many! His insights and support soon proved vital for the further development of the PCR. He became my confidant, and together we went through many storms. I had no idea then that he was to become Blake's successor in 1972.

Philip Potter: A source of inspiration

Potter was a man of the Bible and he reminded his colleagues often of some of the key words to be found there. One of those was "righteousness," which means to be straight, firm, steel-like. To be just is to be right, acting according to one's inner being, he said. Security is about being able to trust one another: mutual trust. And justice is related to fruitful soil and the right use of creation. God's gift of justice is also our work, because we are made in his image. And so racial justice, solidarity with the poor, human rights, and the focus on a truly new community of women and men are part of what the ecumenical movement is about.

I felt continuously inspired by Potter. In working with him, we tried to relate the agenda of the churches to the agenda of the world. We had to invent and tread new ground. And we knew it was a risky undertaking. We tried to work for what later became Potter's call (at the 1983 Vancouver assembly) to become "truly a house of living stones, built on the rock of faith."[3]

After the 1968 Uppsala assembly, we knew we had a mission and we believed that we were on the journey to the Promised Land. But seven years later, after the close of the 1975 Nairobi assembly, Potter assembled his colleagues for a post-mortem and reminded us that we were back in the wilderness, in the desert. The political and ecumenical climate was worsening. And the very churches that had given a mandate to the WCC to take the leadership role were no longer willing to engage in the costly sacrifices they were asked to make. In fact, one might ask whether they had fully understood what they were asking when they made their far-reaching decisions during and after Uppsala.

I remember vividly the many times I went to see Philip Potter in his office of general secretary when most colleagues had already gone home. I was often in despair and frustration about developments in the PCR because some member churches refused to understand the issues and to move with us in an effort to expose the underlying causes of racism and injustice. I badly needed Potter's help because I didn't know how to proceed. Potter would listen to me patiently and then say, "Well, let's first have a little drink." He would open his cupboard and take out a bottle of something, and before tackling the problems I had mentioned he would put me at ease and we would enjoy being *des compagnons de route* (companions on the way) together. He would then tell me wisely to take myself a little less seriously! His style was that of real collegiality: humbly to struggle together to discover the answers to our problems. His authority stemmed from his collegiality. Never did I sense a *diktat* or pressure from above. How different was his style in comparison to that of Visser 't Hooft, an authoritarian "patron" to whom one listened to receive what one had to consider as an order!

Potter helped me to understand what living faith, or rather living out one's faith, is about. But this certainly didn't always make things easier. Often when I entered his office, I sensed how heavy his burden as general secretary was and how lonely one can be in such a position. It was a daunting task. In hindsight I seriously ask myself what would have happened to the Programme to Combat Racism if Philip Potter had not become general secretary.

The search for staff

On 1 January 1970, I started work in my new capacity. I drew up lists of possible candidates for staff and members of the advisory committee. Blake reminded me that he wanted quick action. There was no time to lose!

Archie Le Mone, a black American colleague in the WCC Youth department, suggested I consider for staff Nawaz (Dag) Dawood, a lawyer from the then Ceylon, currently teaching at the London School of Economics. Not totally surprising, he happened to be in the building, and so he came to see me. He struck me as intelligent, shrewd, and full of interesting ideas on how to start the programme running. But he was a Trotskyite and an agnostic, two characteristics that were likely to raise eyebrows among WCC leadership. However, I recommended to Blake that he be appointed. I was under pressure to start working out a programme and could not possibly do this on my own. In fact, though I was in charge (of what?), I was painfully aware that I depended largely on those I still had to find as future colleagues. Blake felt that Dag ought to be interviewed by the moderator and vice-moderator of central committee, M. M. Thomas and Pauline Webb; after that interview, they agreed to his appointment on condition that he be the research secretary with low visibility. Thus Dag soon moved to Geneva and became my first colleague in the PCR.

After a couple of months our team was completed with the appointment as programme secretary of the Rev. Charles Spivey, a black American and executive director of the department of social justice of the National Council of the Churches of Christ in the US. He had participated in the Notting Hill consultation. Originally, the PCR was placed under the direct responsibility of the general secretary, but later it was integrated into a unit grouping other programmes concerned with justice and service. (This also meant that the international advisory committee changed its name to the commission on the Programme to Combat Racism.)

Pauline Webb

Among the members of the PCR commission, Pauline Webb stood out as one of the most inventive and committed to the struggle for racial justice, always ready to give support. As a lay person in the British Methodist Church, she had campaigned for the ordination of women, and as the first woman vice-moderator of the WCC central committee, she showed that she was not afraid of controversy. She was also the first woman and lay person to head religious broadcasting for the BBC World Service: she inspired many around the world through her compassionate meditations in response to world events.

Webb actively participated in the Notting Hill consultation, which laid the foundations for PCR. Afterwards, as I have already said, she defended with conviction its recommendations in the WCC executive and central committees in face of strong objections, choosing to defend the recommendations with the Hebrew word *dabar*, meaning both divine action and prophetic exhortation. "The word of God happened to us," she said. She was driven by her strong biblical faith, so it was only natural that she should become a member of the PCR advisory committee.

For me personally she became a constant help. I would regularly consult her on how to handle difficult matters. One example was how to reject an application for the Special Fund from the leader of the Rhodesian Selous Scouts, a para-military unit part of the white regime under Ian Smith. Cynically, the colonel in charge asked for funds for the construction of a chapel so his soldiers could better meditate on how to wipe out what he called "black terrorists"!

But she took the lead particularly in answering the flow of critical letters to editors of the British press, strongly protesting against the first WCC grants to liberation movements. The PCR was put "on trial" during a BBC radio programme, and Webb was made the defendant against a well-known Anglican priest and friend of South Africa, who was the prosecutor. Together with David Haslam, she began "End Loans to South Africa," a campaign against banks that used street theatre, distributed leaflets to customers, and exercised shareholder action by presenting resolutions at the banks' annual meetings. Her sharp pen was of immense help to us in the PCR, and also in drafting resolutions on Southern Africa for presentation to the central committee. Most important, Webb kept her good humour during PCR committee meetings when things became rough.

The search for advisory committee members

My next responsibility was to produce a list of names for an international advisory committee. We needed an African chairman, and after prolonged search Bola Ige from Nigeria accepted the position in 1971. A lawyer and governor of Oyo Province in Nigeria, he had been one of the "radicals" at the 1966 Church and Society conference. Also, he had long been the general secretary of the Student Christian Movement in Nigeria. Later he became minister of justice in the federal Nigerian government and took a strong position against corruption and crime in his country, which made him many enemies. In 2001, after he left the commission, he was assassinated at his home in Abuja by a group of gangsters.

When chairing committee meetings, he used his lawyer's skill to find a compromise between the members' sometimes very differing opinions. But when he spoke out personally on race issues, he became the radical he was at the 1966 conference. And when he led the committee's morning prayers – which he loved to do – he suddenly used the medieval language of the Anglican *Common Book of Prayer*. I never understood why, but I suspect that despite his strong anti-colonialism, something of a previous era had stayed in his mind.

A key criterion for choosing members of the committee was that two-thirds should be from the third world or from racially oppressed groups. But to find a good balance between continents proved complicated. Because of the programme emphasis on Southern Africa, it was essential for that region to be well represented. Blake felt there should be one white person from South Africa on the committee (a black person would not be allowed by the government to serve), and Alex Boraine, a minister from the Methodist Church, was nominated. But he never felt at ease in the committee; he resigned in the early 1970s and was not replaced.

Early meetings and difficult situations

The first meeting of the committee was held in May 1970, and began with an incident. In the absence of a chair, Blake had asked Pauline Webb to preside the meeting, with the result that there were three white persons at the head table: Webb, Blake, and I. This caused the black American committee member Andy Young to object at the opening, "Let's begin by getting rid of the racism at the top table here, where we are faced by an American bureaucrat, a Dutch layman and Queen Victoria sitting in the chair!" The meeting was then briefly interrupted in order to get the situation sorted out. The incident was a gift for NBC-TV, which had come from the US to film a working day in the life of the WCC general secretary.

Another exciting moment was when one of the committee members, Joyce Clague, an Aboriginal woman from Australia, asked that her baby daughter be baptized during the meeting by Philip Potter, who was then director of the Commission on World Mission and Evangelism (CWME). Symbolically, this was a truly great event.

One of the members, and a "locomotive" of the PCR committee, was Rein-Jan van der Veen (1921-2004) from the Netherlands. With his creative mind he initiated many projects, especially those geared to fund-raising. He had a gift for using the media to expose racism. This meant that churches were often openly put under pressure to show their real colours, for or against combating racism. As the general secretary of the Dutch Missionary Council, he used his influence to confront the Dutch churches with their history in South Africa and the need now to show their support for the black people and their struggle for liberation. The time for (endless) dialogue with the white South African churches was over, he said.

Van der Veen also created the Dutch action group Prepaid Reply, and negotiated substantial support from the Dutch government for the Special Fund. At that time the economist Jan Pronk (well known in the WCC) was government minister for development cooperation. Van der Veen's style was rigorous and his courage in engaging in controversial debates with church and political leaders at home and abroad was surely inspired by his active participation in the Dutch resistance movement during the Second World War. His ecumenical faith was rooted in the need to show what Christian unity means in practice. Personally, I owe much to his never-failing support and friendship.

Commission meetings were never easy to run. Every member had his or her own particular situation in mind and wanted to go home feeling that something tangible had been achieved for their area.

Cooperation with other organizations was essential and we often invited consultants to our commission meetings to bring us up to date and discuss possibilities of working more closely together. Consultants would also inform us on specific situations. For instance, with regard to Southern Africa we invited Garfield Todd (former prime minister of Southern Rhodesia, who had been kicked out of government by the white electorate for working toward a democracy that would include the entire population, both white and black) and Bishop Abel Muzorewa from Rhodesia-Zimbabwe. Others included Abdul Minty (then a leader of the anti-apartheid campaign in Britain), Zephania Kameeta (a Lutheran pastor from Namibia), Allan Boesak (then studying theology in the Netherlands), Bernard Chidzero of UNCTAD (who later became finance minister in Zimbabwe), and Beyers Naudé of the Christian Institute in South Africa.

During one meeting I ran into an embarrassing situation. Andy Young, one of our commissioners, was also a US congressman and a member of the congressional black caucus. As such, he visited South Africa, and upon his return stated that, as a means to explode the apartheid system from within, he favoured more foreign investment in the country (based on the "Sullivan Principles" – Sullivan was a black American pastor who advocated a code of conduct for businesses, requiring the equal treatment of employees regardless of race). I reported this to our moderator Bola Ige, who told me that I should bring Andy's statement to the attention of the whole commission and ask for its opinion, since the WCC was defending quite the opposite – disinvestment from South Africa. When I did this, several black Americans were upset, particularly because I had brought this up as a (white) staff member. But I felt it was my duty anyway, regardless of who was white or black. After acrimonious debate, it was decided that the PCR moderator would write a letter to Andy Young, explaining that his position was contrary to the WCC's policy and that this raised the question of his future participation in the PCR commission. Bola Ige duly signed the letter and I was asked to hand deliver it to Andy in New York. Which is what I did. Andy was not amused and said he would seriously consider resigning. Soon afterwards, he was appointed US ambassador to the UN by Jimmy Carter.

Another difficult moment in the commission's life was when the PCR's mandate was up for renewal by the WCC central committee. Elisabeth Adler had made her assessment of the first five years of our programme. Her report, in the form of a booklet entitled *A Small Beginning*,[4] left no doubt that we were only just starting and that the continuation of PCR was essential. Our commission was then requested to present an extended plan for the future. Father Paul Verghese, one of the commissioners, accepted to make a draft for discussion by the commission. When the paper was tabled, it turned out that the language he had used was to a large extent military. He had assumed that since we were "combating" racism, we could use more such terminology. However, it was immediately clear that the central committee, of which he was himself a member, would never swallow this and that it would antagonize the member churches. The future of the PCR would then be at risk. In the end, a more moderate version was adopted both by our commission and by the central committee.

A postscript: Letter from my father

About one year after we started the PCR, I received an unexpected letter from my father (my parents divorced after the war). I knew of course of his objections to the work we were doing, and it was a subject we tended to avoid discussing.

But in the letter he used strong language: in fact, he suggested that I immediately stop working for the PCR and leave the WCC altogether. This I should do in my personal interest, as well as in that of my wife and children. It was clear for him that the WCC had diverged from its original goals and had become a leftist (Marxist) organization. For him, the Special Fund to Combat Racism was in fact a means for "terrorist movements" to buy arms for use against the white people in Southern Africa. His difficulty was especially with the issue of violence by the liberation movements. In order to be sure that he understood what was happening in the WCC, he had met with the Rev. J .J. Buskes, a famous "red pastor" of Amsterdam who was well known for his anti-apartheid stance and as a member of the peace movement. A greater difference in outlook between the two men was hardly possible! Buskes confirmed to my father that he had great reservations about supporting liberation movements in Southern Africa.

I was amazed and taken aback, especially because my father, who was a lawyer and whose letters were always very balanced and full of consideration, suddenly used the kind of language of the Amsterdam boulevard newspaper *De Telegraaf.* This was very unlike him. But I knew that communism was really what he was most afraid of, and once that was the subject of discussion he could become very emotional. Since the Potsdam and Yalta agreements at the end of the Second World War, he often said that after Nazism the next worldwide danger and tyranny would be communism. Only in the US would one be safe – and he had once even suggested that we move there.

I showed the letter to my wife, Jet. We both felt ashamed and discouraged that for him it had come to this point. Why had he chosen to put his thoughts on paper rather than discussing it openly with us? Was there some truth in his arguments? The best thing we could now do was to put the letter "on ice," and wait a while rather than react emotionally.

So the letter sat for three weeks in a drawer, and then I wrote back to say that I was very disappointed in his position but that both Jet and I honestly felt that I was involved in doing the right thing and that I would continue my work in the WCC as before. However, I did also say that I understood that for some people of his generation, the recent decisions by the WCC had been difficult to accept. What I realized was that Dutch history with South Africa, and especially our strong bonds with the white Afrikaners, made it difficult for some of them to accept our decisions. What the PCR was saying was that it was now time to support the black majority of the country, which had never been taken into consideration by the white minority and had been exploited and oppressed for centuries. My father and his conservative outlook were part of what we had to come to terms with, not only in the Netherlands but in many parts of Europe with its colonial past. The WCC, which had its origins in the Anglo-Saxon world, had grown to maturity now that it was no longer representing mostly churches of the West but included churches from around the world.

Later, just before he had a stroke, my father and I agreed to disagree. We were reconciled when he said to me that regardless of our differences of opinion, he had great respect for my integrity.

7. Priorities and Staff Relations: 1970-1981

The Special Fund to Combat Racism

At the outset, the international advisory committee quickly decided on a number of priorities. It felt that every important decision in the PCR's work should be confirmed by the highest authorities of the WCC to ensure that the council as a whole stood behind the PCR's policies and was answerable for their implementation.

The advisory committee confirmed a strong emphasis on combating worldwide white racism, particularly in Southern Africa. South Africa had been plunged into a deep crisis because of the tense confrontation between an arrogant privileged white minority and a poor oppressed black majority. A country that had the potential of being a living example of a multiracial society had refused to be that example. A white Caucasian minority that claimed to be the last bastion of Christian civilization instead became the purveyors of violence by developing a theological justification of racism-apartheid. It blessed injustices, canonized the will of the powerful, and reduced the poor to passivity and obedience. It misused theological and biblical concepts. Understandably, the WCC's Uppsala assembly and the central committee therefore decided that this situation needed priority attention by the PCR.

The emphasis on South Africa was to be demonstrated immediately through the recommendations to be made for the first grants of the Special Fund created by the 1969 central committee in Canterbury. However, the development of criteria for the distribution of the fund were left to the seven members of the executive group of the advisory committee, which met in Limuru, Kenya, just before the crucial September 1970 meeting of the WCC executive committee in Arnoldshain, West Germany, at which the first grants were made.

When I introduced the first recommendations for grants at Arnoldshain, there were many questions from members of the executive committee. They wanted more detailed descriptions of the organizations proposed to receive grants. These I gave orally. But it was clear that several members were astounded and alarmed by the radical proposals to include Southern African liberation movements. However, Gene Blake and Pauline Webb strongly defended the recommendations, and in the end the whole list was adopted without change. Only the member of the German churches had absented himself when the vote took place.

The criteria did not only stipulate that the grants were to be used for humanitarian purposes. Most important was to strengthen the organizational capability of the racially oppressed people, as well as the absence of control of the manner in which the grants were spent. We had clearly in mind that this last criterion – the matter of control – should be considered as a matter of principle for the WCC as a whole, and in particular for interchurch aid as the WCC's main financial agency in carrying out its many projects around the world. We felt that either we trusted the recipients in their work, or we shouldn't support them. We were probably too optimistic. As far as I am aware, the Special Fund philosophy of trust and no control did not become a general policy of the WCC as we had hoped.

The acceptance of the criteria and the first grants by the WCC executive made headlines worldwide. In South Africa, the announcement unleashed an avalanche of anger from the white establishment both in the church and in politics. The prime minister, John Vorster, immediately made a speech in parliament condemning the WCC for its support of terrorist groups to buy arms, and told the South African member churches to denounce the council. These churches complained they had not been informed in advance of the grants to be made. In fact, church leaders would not have wanted to be associated with the WCC action for fear of a backlash at home. But the general secretary of the South African Council of Churches and the South African member of the PCR committee had both been informed about the impending grants: neither reacted.

On the other hand, Beyers Naudé, the director of the Christian Institute, pleaded for an understanding of the WCC's decisions. He was the only church person in South Africa who, after the announcement of the grants, had the courage to make a statement. He called attention to the

> silence of more than 18 million voices of the black population of South Africa ... They dare not express what they really feel ... The more violent the reaction on the part of the whites, the more convinced did the non-whites become that their salvation from the slavery of apartheid will not come from the white Pharaohs but that they can only expect it from a Moses from their own ranks who at some time ("God alone knows when," as one of them put it) would speak the liberating word and perform the liberating deed.[1]

The crucial point, for Naudé, was not the opinion of the Pretoria government or of the white churches, but of the black majority in South Africa. Although black people could not express themselves openly without risking arrest, he had met enough black leaders in- and outside the black churches to know that in their opinion the WCC's grants were a sign of hope.

In the West, the WCC was immediately accused of one-sidedness in its emphasis on white racism and on Southern Africa, and was heavily criticized for supporting violence through grants to liberation movements. Western media did not distinguish between the armed struggle of some of the liberation movements and their humanitarian programmes. Particularly in Britain the secular and church-related press spoke of "blood money" and of money for murderous Marxist-oriented terrorists. The London *Times* had an interesting editorial comment: it said the action showed that the WCC had come to the pessimistic conclusion that the race problem could not be solved by non-violent transformation. Other London papers reacted very violently to the WCC's grants. The West German radio comment was fair: it raised the question whether the WCC's decision did not call for a rethinking by the Federal Republic of Germany of its trade and other involvement in South Africa. The reaction of the British, West German, and some American churches was violent. The British Council of Churches and Christian Aid washed their hands of any support for the WCC's decision.

But there was a good deal of support as well, notably in messages from the AACC and from President Kaunda of Zambia; and just as importantly there were informal signs of support from black people in South Africa itself, both in- and outside the churches; invariably, however, they did not want to be quoted for fear of reprisals.

The basic underlying concept of the Special Fund was that of a redistribution of power. "There can be no justice in our world without a transfer of economic resources to undergird the redistribution of political power and to make cultural self-determination meaningful."[2] The smallness of the first sums distributed ($200,000 to 19 organizations) underlined the symbolic value of such a "redistribution of power." But it was nevertheless a clear and recognizable ecumenical sign of solidarity instead of the usual charity. Between 1970 and 1990, some US$9.2 million dollars were granted by the Special Fund to organizations in different parts of the world, focusing mainly on Southern Africa.

The first opportunity to test the views of the member churches about the grants came at the central committee at its 1971 meeting in Addis Abeba. It turned out that there was considerable support for the WCC's policy – and not only from churches in the so-called third world. Committee members from North America and from Western and Eastern Europe were on the whole supportive, as was the Russian Orthodox Church. But there were questions, which centred mainly on three issues: Did the WCC, by its actions, support violence? Why were the grants made without control of the manner in which they were spent? Should the WCC risk one-sidedness by concentrating so much of its attention on racism in Southern Africa?

Finally, the churches, through the WCC's central committee, made a crucial statement that clearly showed that the council had entered a new era by expressing Christian concern and support for the victims of oppression. The central committee stated:

> The churches must always stand for the liberation of the oppressed and of victims of violent measures which deny basic human rights. [The CC] calls attention to the fact that violence is in many cases inherent in the maintenance of the status quo. Nevertheless, the WCC does not and cannot identify itself completely with any political movement, nor does it pass judgment on those victims of racism who are driven to violence as the only way left to them to redress grievances and so open the way for a new and more just social order.[3]

This motion, drafted with the help of Ernest Payne (Baptist, UK) and adopted without dissent and no recorded abstentions, helped considerably to put the grants by the Special Fund into perspective. It was interesting that the grants were supported by the so-called peace churches, which condemn any form of violence, while representatives of some of the churches with a history of supporting national wars were strongly opposed to supporting the liberation movements. Equally important was the decision to further implement what was known as "the Martin Luther King resolution" on nonviolent methods of achieving social change, adopted at the Uppsala assembly. The report that was received by the committee said, among other things, that there was:

a growing unwillingness to condemn categorically those groups, including Christians, which resort to violence in the face of situations of massive, entrenched social, racial and economic injustice. Many have spoken of "the violence of the status quo"—that is, the suffering and death which result from unjust social structures when they are not effectively challenged. Others have pointed out that "nonviolence"(either because it is ineffective in a given situation, or precisely because it *is* effective) may have a more violent long-term impact than some of its advocates recognize.[4]

While we were in Addis Abeba, I received the visit of a delegation from Yasser Arafat's Palestinian Liberation Organization (PLO). They had heard of the Special Fund and submitted an application for support. Obviously, taking sides in the Palestine-Israel conflict was a hot issue and likely to divide the WCC's constituency deeply. After discussion with Gene Blake and the Churches' Commission on International Affairs (CCIA), I made clear to the Palestinians that the PLO would not qualify under the criteria of the Fund.

A few years later, we receive an equally curious application for the Special Fund from the Inkatha Freedom Party, signed by Gatsha Buthelezi as the chief minister of his Bantustan. It was clear that the WCC would not consider supporting Bantustans even if the expression "freedom movement" was used in the application. We knew enough about Buthelezi's policies and his dependence on the apartheid regime in Pretoria. But he insisted, and announced his visit to the WCC. Neither the general secretary, Philip Potter, nor the CCIA staff was available, so PCR staff met with Buthelezi and his secretary. After some niceties and coffee, he solemnly read the application to us and then wanted to discuss the details. I interrupted him and said that we had considered his letter and come to the conclusion that Inkatha would not quality. This infuriated him: he took the application, tore it up in front of us, grabbed his chieftain-stick from the table and told his secretary to leave with him. That was the end of a short but memorable meeting.

One of the most difficult aspects of the Special Fund was how to select the organizations and movements that should receive support and determine the amount. In order to make sure that the grants were made in the name of the WCC as a whole, the PCR executive recommended the list of grants to the WCC's executive committee for final decision. Because combating white racism in Southern Africa was priority number one, we needed to solicit applications from that area. Grants would be made only on the basis of well-documented applications. So we sent letters to different movements alerting them to the existence of the fund. Some reacted immediately; others whom we considered crucial kept silent, for example, the ANC. We all remembered Chief Albert Luthuli, a great South African and one of the ANC's first presidents.[5] He died in 1967 after mysteriously being run over by a train. At Luthuli's funeral, the writer Alan Paton said of him,

> They took away his chieftainship, but he never ceased to be chief. They took away his temporal power, but he never ceased to have his spiritual power. They took away his freedom, but he never ceased to be free. He was indeed more free than those who bound him.[6]

Consequently, we had to make repeated contacts with the ANC. The problem was probably related to its bad internal administrative organization at the time, which was divided between its offices in the frontline states and in London. In the end, the ANC's first application was made through the (London-based) Luthuli Memorial Foundation for scholarships. On the other hand, the Pan Africanist Congress of Azania (PAC), an organization that split off from the ANC and that claimed to be more revolutionary, usually sent only very summary applications. One year, when no details were forthcoming before the deadline, we decided against making a grant to them. This caused a furore and the PAC sent a delegation to Geneva demanding an explanation. They simply considered that they were entitled to an annual grant, full stop! We had to explain that there was no such right and that consideration would only be given on the basis of detailed applications.

In the case of South Africa, Mozambique, Angola, Namibia, and Zimbabwe, there was the added problem that for political reasons we could not officially contact the national Christian councils of churches concerned for advice.

For Angola, we were faced with applications from three rival liberation movements: the People's Movement for the Liberation of Angola (MPLA), the Revolutionary Government of Angola in Exile (GRAE), and the National Union for the Total Independence of Angola (UNITA). It was known that on some occasions these movements were not only fighting the Portuguese colonialists but also each other, which considerably complicated our task. But we were greatly helped by the liberation committee of the Organization of African Unity (OAU), which advised us on the capacity and reliability of the different movements. This is not to say that we rubber-stamped their opinion. Clearly, there were strategic, political, and ideological considerations that influenced the OAU's advice and to a certain extent also the PCR's recommendations for grants. Thus, it was well known that the PAC policy was anti-white and "blacks only" ("one Boer, one bullet," was one of their slogans). Nevertheless, in order to keep some necessary balance, and bearing in mind existing sensitivities among churches and missions involved in those countries, grants would sometimes be made to competing movements, though not necessarily in the same amount.

Several liberation movement leaders came to visit us regularly. This was the occasion for them to meet not only PCR staff but also the general secretary and other WCC staff colleagues, especially in CCIA and the Africa secretary in interchurch aid. Most of the leaders were Christians, educated by Roman Catholic or Protestant missions. They wanted to know why the WCC was suddenly interested in their plight. We, on the other hand, wanted to know about their ideology and their policies and methods of liberation. How did they see the future of their country? Some leaders were open-minded, admitting enormous problems in keeping their movement together because of internal dissension and outside pressure by donor agencies. They would also report on infiltration by the colonial regimes and efforts to destroy their movement. Others were more cautious and diplomatic, limiting their discussions with us to finding out about future PCR support. On the whole, it can be said that these meetings contributed considerably to trust-building, which we considered important for the future role of the churches in those countries.

It turned out that only a few WCC member churches had knowledge of liberation movements in Southern Africa and their *raison d'être*. One way of informing them was for the PCR to draw up, publish, and widely distribute profiles on some of these movements. These profiles also proved useful in answering the thousands of enquiries we received from individuals all over the world after the first grants were made. They helped us to overcome a first period when we were clearly put on the defensive because of the outcry by the South African member churches, as well as prime minister Vorster's claim that the WCC was involving itself in violence and supporting "terrorist movements, killing innocent people."

One particularly difficult issue when making grants to liberation movements in South Africa was the position of the WCC's member churches in that country. Normally they should have been consulted before any such crucial decision concerning them and their country was taken. The decision not to involve them represented a shift in the WCC's thinking. The churches in South Africa had on the whole not been part of the resistance to the apartheid system in the 1950s and 1960s, and it was felt that they no longer represented the aspirations of the oppressed majority in the country. The WCC-sponsored Cottesloe consultation in 1960, following the Sharpeville massacre, had been an effort to remedy this by trying to draw the churches out of isolation and engage them in facing apartheid together. But the meeting caused sharp conflict between the Dutch Reformed Churches and the English-speaking churches. As a result, two white Dutch Reformed Churches, under strong pressure from the apartheid government, left the WCC. Church leaders rejecting apartheid – like Trevor Huddleston, Joost de Blank, Ambrose Reeves, and later Beyers Naudé – were the exceptions in that period. Thus, advance disclosure of the WCC's intentions was no longer advisable. After a serious crisis of conscience, in fact, Beyers Naudé, a former moderator of the Dutch Reformed Church of Transvaal and originally an important member of the secret Afrikaner Broederbond to which all government ministers belonged, launched with others the Christian

Institute, a non-racial body, which placed him at the forefront of the ecumenical movement in South Africa. Consequently, he was forced to leave the ministry of his church, and he became one of the most prominent opponents of apartheid. He died in 2004 and was given a state funeral.

The WCC was facing a situation in South Africa that was considered of extreme urgency worldwide. The UN and various other world bodies had taken position and were acting. But the churches in South Africa itself, which had been co-responsible for the development of apartheid, could not be considered as partners in the struggle for justice. Their involvement would come only later. During this period, the dominant influence of the state and the Broederbond on the thinking of the churches was enormous. Thus, in hindsight one might say that it was the impulse from abroad and in particular the action of the WCC that brought, or rather forced, the South African churches to start facing their common responsibility.

Relations with liberation movements in Southern Africa

As PCR staff we had to deal with a variety of personalities in the liberation movements. Some of these relations turned sour; others were more fruitful.

At one point, the WCC executive committee, at our recommendation, decided not to make an annual grant to the Revolutionary Government of Angola in Exile (GRAE). Their leaders, and particularly Roberto Holden, were furious. They sent a delegation of five to Geneva and demanded an explanation from Blake, who accepted to receive them at his home during the evening. We were prepared to explain our decision, but GRAE used such belligerent language that it became impossible to have any reasonable discussion. Obviously the issue was one of competition with the two other Angolan movements, MPLA and UNITA, which did receive grants. Our information had been that GRAE was in disarray and trying to destroy the other movements. After forty-five minutes of shouting, the delegation left dissatisfied and angry.

Another story, but of a different and more positive nature, was when on the eve of the 1976 Geneva talks (initiated by the UK) between the parties in the Rhodesia/Zimbabwe conflict, Philip Potter gathered the leaders of the four liberation movements taking part in the negotiations for an evening dinner at the WCC. Joshua Nkomo, Robert Mugabe, Abel Muzorewa, and Ndabaningi Sithole had not seen each other for years, and two of them had only just been released from prison. In fact, they had become strangers to each other. We knew that unless they had at least some common purpose and understanding of the main issues and pitfalls at the outset of the meeting, they would be an easy target for a divide-and-rule game by Ian Smith and his white cronies, who were still the leaders of white Rhodesia.

Staff of PCR and International Affairs fetched the leaders by car from their respective hotels. But Nkomo suddenly left for a meeting with President Mobutu of Zaire at his vacation villa near Lausanne. So we had to settle for his deputy. This was an embarrassing incident but very much part of working with liberation movements. Table arrangements had been made in such a way that WCC staff sat in between the four leaders, who looked at each other with stony faces. Sensing the mood, Potter, in his inimitable Caribbean style, made a few jokes and told a few stories, and slowly the ice began to melt. Then he asked whether the WCC could be of any help logistically or otherwise to them during the negotiations that were to start the next morning at the UN. After a silence, Comrade Sithole raised his hand and hesitatingly asked for a typewriter and some carbon paper in order to be able to type his speech for the opening ceremony of the conference. There was general laughter and the dinner became less formal.

But the real discussion did not take place until we staff were taking the four back to their hotels in town. As we walked to the car park, suddenly the four gentlemen disappeared into the dark. The Swiss security officials became extremely nervous and asked whether we had seen where they went. We hadn't. About twenty minutes later they reappeared with smiles on their faces. As we drove them to their hotels they told us, "We have talked and agreed on what we are going to say at the opening of the conference tomorrow." Perhaps this was one of the small contributions the WCC could make to their finding a joint strategy facing their common enemy.

Ending bank loans to South Africa

We gradually learned that action with a specific and well-defined focus usually stood a far better chance of achieving its aims than action that was general and unspecific. International bank loans in support of the white regime were a cornerstone to the maintenance of the system of apartheid. Churches all over the world could use their influence to end such loans, and making this understandable to Christians was one of the WCC's responsibilities. The WCC, because it had to speak and act in the name of its member churches on these delicate and complicated issues of finance, had to choose its course very carefully, both adopting a strategy that could command widespread agreement and addressing itself to those institutions whose role had been quite ambiguous.

To me, ending bank loans to and disinvestment from South Africa was a far more crucial and profound element of PCR's policy than the issue of financial support to the liberation movements. It called into question the very capitalist system that undergirded Western society and its churches.

Historically speaking, it is particularly interesting to note that the International Missionary Council (IMC) was one of the first ecumenical bodies to explore the challenges Christianity faced in a modern capitalist society. Already at its Jerusalem conference in 1928, the IMC underscored the problems presented by "the investment of capital in undeveloped areas and the necessity of securing that it take place on terms compatible with the welfare and progress of indigenous peoples."[7] It spoke of the obligation of governments of the economically more advanced countries to ensure that economically less developed people are protected against economic and social injustice and share fully and equitably in the fruits of economic progress.

In 1938, at its meeting in Tambaram, the IMC scrutinized its own economic practices in light of its mission:

> A church which proclaims a gospel which transcends all distinction of race, class and nation must take scrupulous care lest it deny that gospel by any policy or act savouring of racial, class or national arrogance. Here we wish to draw attention to the importance of the way in which church funds are invested.[8]

Tambaram cautioned that churches seeking a substantial income may be "tempted to invest their endowments or other trust funds in enterprises that are unworthy" or "not consistent with the things for which the churches stand."[9] The contradiction of making verbal statements against racism while supporting economic systems fostering racial discrimination was clearly highlighted and it remained a major issue within the WCC right from its founding in 1948.

Philip Potter, who never ceased to remind us of the history of the ecumenical movement, was the first to draw our attention to what the IMC had already seen. Gene Blake had the courage in 1969 to make the WCC start transforming words into deeds. And when Blake left in 1972, Potter as the new general secretary bore the brunt of all the criticism of the PCR by the more powerful (white) member churches. In fact, we had only been implementing what they had themselves decided the WCC should be doing.

The issue of ending bank loans led to very heated discussions both in- and outside the churches between two different points of view. One was that economic growth of South Africa through more investment would help explode the apartheid system from within. This was also the usual opinion of financial institutions and multinationals. It was shared by many in the Western churches, who felt that boycott and disinvestment would lead to greater poverty of the black population, whose liberation was the objective of the WCC's action. On the other hand, the WCC, together with the worldwide anti-apartheid movement and many national and local ecumenical councils and groups, defended the position that investment reinforced the apartheid system. The Pretoria regime depended heavily on foreign financial support. Cutting that support would weaken the regime, and support the movement for liberation and a negotiated settlement.

The PCR insisted that it would listen first and foremost to the voices of the oppressed black people. And with time these voices became louder in demanding that Western support for the liberation process include economic pressure. Meanwhile, not only the ANC but also the South African Council of Churches (SACC) was on record as supporting economic and other sanctions to influence a change of regime.

But banks and multinationals defended themselves by insisting that their policies were not influenced by political motivation. They were unable or unwilling to see the relation between economic and political ends, and especially so in the case of South Africa. Our reasoning was that the West and its capitalist system were complicit in maintaining apartheid. The WCC appealed especially to the ethical responsibility of the banks. For the WCC, capital could only be a means to achieve a goal, while for the banks, capital was a goal in itself. In the end this led the WCC to decide to close its accounts with several of its banks.

The finance department, through its director Frank Northam, had at the very beginning expressed strong reservations about using part of the WCC's reserves for the launching of the Special Fund. Later on, it objected fiercely to any decision to cut the WCC's relations with banks making loans to the South African government. The general secretary and the WCC executive committee had to intervene in order to make the finance department follow overall WCC policies.

The WCC decided to concentrate largely, though not exclusively, on the European-American Banking Corporation (EABC) and its member banks. EABC had a unique connection with South Africa. It made substantial credit arrangements and a concerted effort to assist the government of South Africa in overcoming its serious economic and financial problems. The WCC sent an explanatory document to the EABC and its members, soliciting assurances that they would stop granting loans to the South African government and its agencies. If such assurances were not forthcoming, no more WCC funds would be deposited with these banks. At the same time, the WCC urged its member churches to use their influence to press these and other banks participating in loans to stop doing so.

In a letter to one of the EABC members, the AMRO Bank in the Netherlands, the WCC wrote,

> Capital itself is morally neutral, because only a society which consumed everything it produced could avoid the accumulation of capital (whether liquid or in fixed assets), and such a society would betray future generations. What can never be morally neutral, however, is the use to which capital is put. So while banking as an activity is common to many societies, the particular policies which it chooses to adopt are a proper object of moral judgment ... Because it is central to the gospel that faith without works is dead, churches individually – and as grouped in the WCC – owe their primary loyalty not to their own members but to the Lord of the *oikoumene*, the whole inhabited earth ... This has some very concrete practical implications for the World Council... [The WCC has] to see that any capital for which it has responsibility is used for its God-given purpose. That purpose is not the accumulation of more capital, but self-giving service in the name of its self-giving Lord ... So capital is for WCC a means, while for AMRO, it appears to be an end in itself.[10]

The correspondence with the banks brought into the open the issue of public accountability, an issue which neither the banks nor the churches had faced in such an acute form. It highlighted the usefulness of multiple strategies, including discussions with banks as well as boycotts and closing bank accounts, the importance of the educational aspect of ecumenical action, and the need for strategies to combat racism on an institutional and not just on an individual level. The banking issue showed that racism can be no less real when its roots are in supposedly neutral structures run by people without racial prejudice.

A particularly difficult decision was to cut relations in 1981 with three of the WCC's major banks which were heavily involved in loans to the South African government: the Dresdner Bank, the Swiss Bank Corporation (SBS), and the Union Bank of Switzerland (UBS). The PCR, together with the general secretary and the finance department, worked out carefully defined criteria for assessing the involvement of the WCC's own banks active in South Africa. These criteria were adopted by the WCC executive committee in February 1981 and conveyed to the banks concerned. Later, Philip Potter held a special press conference on the issue and explained in detail the WCC's position, announcing the termination of its relationships with these three banks. He explained that the WCC was not in any way criticizing the services rendered by these banks, nor their employees, but the policy they followed in relation to South Africa. The breaking of relations was in order to "express the WCC's full support to the liberation of South Africa from the system of racism embodied in apartheid."[11]

On paper this sounded like a logical decision, but one should not underestimate the enormous power and influence of these banks. The Swiss and German churches that were also clients of these banks opposed the WCC decision. At the same time, however, these churches were the financial supporters of major aspects of the WCC's programmes! Potter took responsibility for a daring decision – all the more so because finding alternative banking with a similar worldwide network proved far from easy.[12]

By the mid-1970s, disinvestment and boycott policies had already for several years been developed by the Interfaith Center on Corporate Responsibility (ICCR) in the US under the leadership of Timothy Smith. It was extremely important for the PCR to be able to point to existing church-sponsored examples. In Europe and also in Australia and New Zealand this kind of ethical involvement by churches in the world of finance and economics was unheard of. Yet it was part of our responsibility to uncover and reveal the realities of the financial world as these related to apartheid and racism.

An early assessment goes up in smoke

Just before the WCC's assembly in Nairobi in 1975, the executive committee met to go over the assembly programme and discuss any urgent matters. A year earlier it had asked the PCR to produce a document to show the extent to which individual member churches, mainly in the West, had taken seriously the various recommendations made by the WCC on disinvestment, bank loans, and white emigration to South Africa. The results of the study could then be shared with the assembly in Nairobi. Since this was a major undertaking, I had asked Gilbert Rist of the Europe-Third World Centre in Geneva to take overall responsibility for the project and apportion the study to various countries. Together we agreed on a consultant in each country who would assemble the information and evaluate the results. The study was ready just in time and we shipped some 2000 copies to Nairobi.

Philip Potter, who had written a short introduction, thought it important to inform the members of the WCC executive and tabled this for the closing session. I was not a little surprised when suddenly several members got together in a corner. When the session opened committee members – including Jacques Rossel, Ernest Payne, Visser 't Hooft, and Richard von Weiszäcker – strongly criticized the booklet, arguing that the researchers in different countries had not been appointed with the blessing of the member churches or of the national councils of churches. Who were these researchers to criticize openly the member churches for not having lived up to the WCC's recommendations? The discussion was so vehement that Potter had no alternative but to withdraw the study and ask me to collect the copies already distributed in the meeting.

It was then decided not only that there was to be no distribution at the assembly, but that all copies should be burned by the stewards under the guidance of Jürgen Hilke, director of WCC Communication. I was furious because I had not even been given the chance to explain and defend the booklet. But I had no alternative, and collected the copies around the table. I am probably not mistaken that never in the history of the WCC had a study gone up in smoke. It made me think of the Vatican's tradition of putting books on the index and consequently burning them.

The next day one of the stewards gave me a copy of the photograph he took of the burning as a testimony for the PCR records. I zealously keep that picture, together with some copies of the study which I saved. And the study is now available in the WCC library![13] I must admit that I did not select the most conservative researchers I could find: Why should I? But for some members of the executive committee, I clearly went too far. They were no doubt afraid of the possible backlash in their own churches.

WCC cooperation with the UN and secular NGOs

It seems extraordinary that in one and the same year, 1948, three major developments took place. First, the UN Human Rights Charter was signed (marked by the conspicuous absence of South Africa and the Soviet Union amongst the signatories). Second, in South Africa, in a traumatic experience for black people, the Nationalist Party, led by D. F. Malan (a sometime minister of the Dutch Reformed Church), came to power and instituted the policy of "apartheid." And third, the WCC was formally created, which became the major expression of the ecumenical movement in the 20th century.

Both the UN and the WCC were almost immediately confronted with the issue of racism as one of the major problems confronting the unity of humankind. The UN concentrated on decolonization and also created a special committee on apartheid. It met regularly in Geneva. As to the churches' concern over racism, this pre-dated the creation of the WCC. Already the 1937 Oxford conference on Life and Work, a landmark in ecumenical thinking, included in its report on "The church and community" a section on the church and race, which set forth the fundamental concepts of Christian race relations for later ecumenical gatherings.

Though the first assembly of the WCC did not take up the race problem as such, the second assembly in Evanston in 1954 could not possibly avoid it because of the mounting crises in the US and in South Africa. At all subsequent WCC assemblies, the issue of racism was one of the predominant concerns.

For a long time, however, there was little or no direct cooperation between the churches' efforts and those of the UN. This changed with the creation of the PCR. We were very conscious that we could not go it alone, especially since we moved from personal, individual forms of race relations to institutional racism. Support to liberation movements and the boycott of banks and multinationals made it necessary to find allies and to cooperate with the UN and NGOs and the world-wide anti-apartheid movement that had already taken initiatives in this direction. Thus the PCR made many contacts with these organizations and largely benefited from the results of their research. It was clear that if the churches and the WCC wanted to make their impact, they needed to cooperate closely with them. The UN on several occasions published our PCR material, including that on the Bantustans and on multinationals and banks.

Furthermore, a number of national anti-apartheid committees applied and received grants from the Special Fund. The PCR tried to encourage the churches in the countries concerned to enter into direct contact with the anti-apartheid movements and support them directly.

Initially, there was some mistrust of the PCR on the part of the anti-apartheid groups as well as the left and the trade unions in general. The left historically considered that the anti-apartheid struggle was its territory and had for years considered the role of the churches as apologetic of apartheid. Christian socialists had of course been an exception; but on the whole, the image of the churches was largely linked to the white pro-apartheid establishment. It seemed to them as if apartheid was both defended and combated in the name of Christian faith.

With the support of the UN special committee on apartheid, many national anti-apartheid movements had taken initiatives, organizing boycotts of South African products and organizations as well as of multinationals operating in the country. The PCR staff made frequent contacts with these movements, and after a while there developed strong cooperation and joint action.

As staff, we frequently received letters telling us that we were villains, that we made a mockery of the gospel, and that churches should disengage from the WCC. We were the devil incarnate, communists, Marxists, and distributed money to evil so-called liberation movements, which were in fact terrorist. Some letters included personal threats: we would be carefully watched and if we didn't change our policies we could be the victims of physical attack. This was strong language and didn't make things easier for us. We wondered who was behind this campaign. But we soon found out that, besides genuine protest and misunderstanding of what we were doing, there were a number of people from different countries who used the same language. This could only be the result of smear campaigns originating in South Africa's propaganda machine, which had branches in different parts of the world. We therefore decided that there was no need to answer these letters.

Changes in staff and division of labour

Within PCR, we were three executive staff and two administrative assistants. We were to develop a worldwide anti-racism programme and do so both through the member churches and their agencies and through ecumenical groups. But opinions within the staff were not unanimous. In fact, racism was also part of relations within and between the PCR staff itself.

Charles Spivey, the black American on our team, following his previous strategy as the executive responsible for anti-racism activities in the US churches, soon took a radical American position in our staff meetings. This was very much in line with prevalent Black Power attitudes in the US, but caused considerable friction not only in the PCR but in the WCC as a whole. In the end, I came to the conclusion that the situation had become untenable and that one of us should leave. At that point I seriously considered resigning. We could not both continue in the same organization without damaging the reputation of both the PCR and ourselves. Blake decided to discuss the matter with the American members of the central committee and Spivey then decided to return to the US, while Edler Hawkins, a black (Presbyterian) American member of central committee, became a temporary consultant with an office in the PCR to help us out. This was the end of an unpleasant struggle. I did certainly not experience Spivey's departure as a victory on my part: rather, it was a defeat for what we thought we stood for – racial justice. Hawkins was experienced, and a trusted person especially in the US, who did justice both to Spivey and to me. He gave good advice and stayed on for a while after Spivey left.

I had to find a successor immediately and decided it would have to be a member of the PCR commission who was already knowledgeable about the programme. José Chipenda from Angola and secretary of the World Student Christian Federation (WSCF) for Africa in Nairobi accepted to become our new secretary for programme and he moved to Geneva in October 1973.

His appointment quieted down the earlier upheavals, and he started a number of important projects in Asia, Australia, and Latin America that considerably widened the spectrum of our actions, while at the same time satisfying the West German and Swiss churches, which still had great difficulty in supporting disinvestment and boycott programmes in Southern Africa.

In 1974, during the WCC central committee in West Berlin, Dag Dawood told me he had had a strange visit at his hotel of two white South Africans who wanted to know why he worked with the WCC and what exactly his responsibilities were in the PCR. It was clear to Dawood that these gentlemen were sent by the Pretoria regime to investigate his background. Some time earlier, he had told me that he might be "found out" as a Trotskyist agnostic and in that case he would have to leave for his own sake and particularly in order to avoid trouble for the WCC. This was a real blow to us all. Though

Dawood had not always been an easy personality to deal with, he had helped considerably by acquainting me with the thinking and writings of revolutionary intellectuals like Malcolm X, Walter Rodney,[14] and Frantz Fanon.[15] Dawood had a good sense of humour and had been very much our "strategist and tactician," developing and writing up most of the proposals for disinvestment and boycott policies submitted subsequently to the PCR commission and to the central committee. Also, he knew how to get in touch with a number of key personalities in the different liberation movements in Southern Africa, which greatly facilitated discussions with them about possible support and grants from the Special Fund.

On the other hand, after the first four years, it was the right time for a change. We had made a very strong (and controversial) start. We had made our point that we were "in business." Words were put into practice as requested by the Uppsala assembly. It was time to deepen and detail our various policies, which required someone with knowledge of church thinking and practices.

Looking for a new research secretary, Pauline Webb, still vice-moderator of the central committee and a very active member of our PCR commission, alerted me to a young British Anglican priest who worked as a religious correspondent for the BBC in London. He was an articulate writer and keen to do research. Alexander (Sandy) Kirby accepted to join the staff on condition that he could remain stationed in London while being most of the week in Geneva. Though this was not ideal, I accepted, and it worked. Kirby became a loyal and critical colleague. As a former BBC correspondent he had a fluent pen. He edited the correspondence between the WCC and banks on loans to the South African government.[16] He also wrote about other key issues, including South Africa's Bantustan policy and its implications for the black people.[17] The booklet answered such questions as: What are the objectives of the Bantustans policy? What are the implications for the black majority? What do black people think? What are the positions of the liberation movements and national and international organizations such as the Organization of African Unity and the United Nations? What have the churches and Christians individually said on the issue?

South Africa's Bantustan policies were then debated in the WCC's central committee, which adopted a resolution condemning the deceptive manoeuvre of the South African government to perpetuate and consolidate apartheid by the creation of the "independent" Transkei, by which three million South Africans were made foreigners in their own country.

With Chipenda, Kirby, and myself as executives and Gisela Gregoriades and Irene Hayertz as administrative assistants, we were a solid team. Gisela was much more than simply an administrative assistant. She protected me when I was under great pressure by answering phone calls and letters on her own initiative, and remained calm when things became hectic and nerves were on edge. When I was discussing PCR policies with (most often) German church groups visiting the WCC, she would sometimes come into the meeting room and tell me that I was urgently wanted somewhere else, giving me the excuse to end the meeting before all the critical questions by the group were answered. Basically, what I said to these groups was that, no, we were not supporting violence in Southern Africa, and that the basic issue was not violence or non-violence but our commitment to the struggle for justice and overcoming fear of change, which we felt was one of the basic problems in many churches.

I knew that only strong teamwork would enable us to weather the many storms we faced. For me as a white person there was no question of "playing" the role of director other than taking responsibility for the overall leadership and coordination. Thus there developed between us a certain division of labour, which meant that each one could develop his or her strong points and obvious responsibilities. Mine was our relationship with member churches, particularly in Europe, and fundraising, as well as maintaining close contact with the anti-apartheid work of the UN. Many churches had expressed considerable reservations about our objectives and the way we wanted to achieve them, so frequent visits to meet with church leaders at the national and local level to explain what we were trying to do were essential. I was travelling nearly all the time, mostly to West Germany, but also to the UK, Scandinavia, the Netherlands, and within Switzerland, as well as to the UN in New York. I also had to give considerable attention to the media, especially the conservative press, which had decided that the WCC had become a Marxist organization.

On several occasions I met with the heads of member churches, trying to explain our policies and programmes. This was not always easy, as I was a layperson and spoke a different language than the theologians I faced. This was particularly the case in West Germany and Switzerland. The Swiss churches live and work in a decentralized manner on a cantonal basis, and the Federation of Protestant Churches in Bern took great care to underline that they had no power to speak on behalf of the cantonal churches. This was one way of avoiding taking a clear position with regard to the PCR. At the same time, however, the Federation maintained strong links with banks and multinationals, who were most critical of the WCC's initiatives, and it often reflected the opinions of the economic and political heavyweights. At one point I had to speak to a large gathering organized by the churches in Zurich and found that my opposite number was a reserve colonel in the Swiss army. He sharply criticized the WCC for supporting rebels and terrorists who tried to topple central authority. Pretoria represented the only legal authority in South Africa and the military were there to defend legitimate power against outside danger. My story about listening to the voices of the powerless and discriminated was not acceptable. The colonel received warm applause, whereas my speech was received in silence and with polite coughing.

In West Germany I met the president of the Evangelical Church in Germany, Bishop Dr Eduard Lohse. He was adamant that the PCR first develop a theology on racism before engaging in action. My reply that we had opted for a theology that would develop "en route" was unacceptable to him. No doubt that the Lutheran theory of the two kingdoms was one of the obstacles to understanding what we were after.[18] True, we parted with a smile, but not exactly as friends.

The church situation in Scandinavia proved very different. The Lutherans were a state church but they warmly supported the Southern African liberation movement, as did their governments. My meetings with the Swedish archbishop of Uppsala and the Finnish archbishop of Helsinki were formal but friendly. The Scandinavian churches supported the Special Fund, and Swedish and Finnish missions in Southern Africa were supportive of the liberation movements.

José Chipenda worked very hard on getting the African churches on board and supportive of our work. Here we were disappointed. Many of the first-generation African church leaders had been trained and educated in the West, but we had not anticipated that many of them would be reluctant openly to take a critical position vis-à-vis churches and theologies of the West, which was implied in a programme to combat *white* racism.

Chipenda was sometimes rather critical of some liberation movements. In this connection it is interesting to note that his brother Daniel was one of the commanders in the Angolan liberation movement UNITA. However, José's comments were particularly, though not exclusively, related to the Zimbabwean movements, which he considered to be out of touch with the people. He felt that the PCR's support to these movements meant that it was not working in the long-term interest of the people. Sandy Kirby, on the other hand, wondered whether the possibility of a first black government in Zimbabwe would represent a victory of the Kissinger doctrine (preservation of Zimbabwe as a sphere for Western exploitation through the creation of a black bourgeoisie) and the likelihood that this might also happen in Namibia.

Another disappointment was the attitude of the black churches in the US. Blake, who had been the key figure in getting the PCR adopted, had strong backing in the big and mainly white American churches. They had been very vocal for the WCC to start the PCR and financial support from them came quickly. But most of the black churches stayed silent. What was more, when we wanted to develop programmes in the US, we found a wall of reluctance among the American churches. It became clear that we were not to get into their backyard! On the other hand, they were in the forefront in backing up our priority programmes in Southern Africa. Support for the liberation movements was less controversial in the US than in the European churches. And WCC disinvestment and boycott policies especially found strong encouragement in black circles.

When Sandy Kirby left in 1977, he was succeeded as research secretary by Prexy Nesbitt, a black American activist with a trade-union background and well known in his country and beyond for his involvement in the anti-apartheid struggle. In a sense he became our new "strategist" after Dag Dawood for developing new WCC policies on racism. Though he lacked a solid church relationship, which was a handicap, he considerably strengthened our ties with the worldwide anti-racist movement. The PCR benefited a great deal from his trade-union and other relations in the US and elsewhere.

1977: South Africa's hope — What price now?

In 1977, the crisis in South Africa reached a new height. Steve Biko, the well-known leader of the Black Consciousness Movement and an emphatically peaceful opponent of apartheid, was killed in police custody, and a month later eighteen organizations, including the Christian Institute of Beyers Naudé, were banned by the South African government.

World opinion was outraged. Many churches, national councils of churches, and regional and world ecumenical bodies, including the WCC, made strong statements of condemnation. Like other people, Christians were bound to ask whether these latest measures were simply a further step in a policy of increasing repression or whether they represented a final stage for the apartheid regime. How were we to interpret the facts, and how were we to respond to them? Among the organizations banned was the newspaper *The World*, South Africa's second largest daily and the one most widely read by black people. The Johannesburg *Financial Mail*, a liberal weekly, commented:

> One thing is certain, Kruger's action has taken South Africa another step away from the possibility of peaceful racial reconciliation and further down the road that leads to violence ... Kruger

may be able to ban and detain who he likes at will. But one thing neither he nor anyone else will ever succeed in doing is banning black South Africans' loathing of apartheid and their determination to be free of it for ever ... Jimmy Kruger may well find that in banning *The World* he has taken on the world. And that world cannot be silenced by a banning order.[19]

PCR staff decided that this was a moment for serious reflection. We produced a background paper entitled "South Africa's Hope – What Price Now?"[20] which was widely circulated among member churches, members of central committee, national councils of churches, and interested groups and individuals. Philip Potter, the general secretary, agreed to its distribution on the condition that it had no official status, but was intended to raise pertinent questions for discussion about future action by the churches. We hoped that these issues would be placed on the agenda of relevant church committees and working groups and that we would receive comments and suggestions for concrete action in supporting the oppressed as they struggled for liberation.

In the background paper, we made clear the principal effects of apartheid. By virtue of its apartheid legislation the white government:

- *Rules by a farcical 'rule of law':* the black population had no say in any of the laws to which it was subject. Moreover, any South African may be detained without trial – and without recourse to the courts – with no time limit at all, and with no access to family or lawyers.
- *Rules by arbitrary definition:* 'terrorism', 'communism', and 'subversion' are three of the labels most commonly used to define any activity of which the government disapproves.
- *Hangs more people than the rest of the Western world put together.*
- *Admits a high number of deaths in detention.*
- *Forbids people of different racial groups to marry or have sexual relations (under the Immorality Act).*

- *Treats all Africans in the white 86 percent of the country as temporary migrants.*
- *Reserves skilled jobs (and others) for whites.*
- *Uses the Bantustans as reservoirs of cheap black labour.*
- *Provides the country's people with racially-segregated health care.*
- *Provides the country's children with racially-segregated education.*
- *Gives white South Africans one of the highest standards of living in the world.*[21]

Every fact cited was taken from authoritative published sources. This catalogue explained why the apartheid policy inspired such massive and desperate opposition. And we argued that perhaps the most important lesson was the realization that the bannings, detentions, and arrests marked not simply a further stage in a policy of increasing repression but that policy's rapid slide toward a final stage. For having outlawed all the remaining peaceful channels for expressing opposition to apartheid, the South African government had served notice that it was prepared to do anything to muzzle its opponents.

The new bannings were to be seen in line with the violent repression of the Soweto youth uprising in June 1976. Through this uprising, young Africans, the apartheid generation, made clear their determination not to live out the rest of their lives under the only system they had ever known. Significantly, their revolt was joined by their coloured and Indian peers, who thus made clear their total rejection of white attempts to divide them from the Africans by offering them marginally better treatment. The initiative for ending apartheid lay with the black people of South Africa, with the support of those whites who could find the courage and vision to join them. Increasingly, the opponents of apartheid inside the country had to choose between keeping silent and engaging in illegal activity.

But the stark choice that now faced South Africans also faced those people outside the country who were determined to see apartheid and exploitation ended. Many had hoped against hope for a sign that South Africa was capable of peaceful change and that they could contribute to the search for a just society through reform. How did that hope stand now, and how were we to respond?

The Lutheran World Federation's assembly in Dar es Salaam in 1977 had recognized that the situation in Southern Africa constituted a *status confessionis*. This meant that, on the basis of faith and in order to manifest the unity of the church, churches would publicly and unequivocally reject the existing apartheid system. Later in that same year, the World Alliance of Reformed Churches made a similar decision. In addition, it expelled two of its white (Afrikaner) Dutch Reformed churches.

It was worth remembering also the distinction that Christians had sometimes made between their person and their office in connection with violence. According to this distinction, there could be a significant difference between violence used for one's self-preservation and violence used in protection of another. The refusal to pass judgment on those who believed they had no option but to answer repressive violence with the violence of rebellion was reflected by the PCR, which had made and continued to make grants from its Special Fund to a number of liberation movements in Southern Africa, including the ANC and the PAC (both of them black peoples' movements banned by the South African government in 1960).

But, we asked in our background paper, can we claim to stand in solidarity with those who rebel for a just cause if we simply refuse to pass judgment on them? The new situation demanded of us far more precision in saying what we meant by a just rebellion. It was important to recall that it was the struggle of a historically non-violent majority against a determined violent minority. We reminded the churches of a report on violence and non-violence commended by the 1973 WCC central committee which stated:

> There are some forms of violence in which Christians may not participate and which the churches must condemn. There are violent causes – the conquest of one people by another or the deliberate oppression of one class or race by another – which offend divine justice. There are violent means of struggle – torture in all forms, the holding of innocent hostages and the deliberate

or indiscriminate killing of innocent combatants, for example – which destroy the soul of the perpetrator as surely as the life and health of the victim.[22]

We did not define as terrorists the resistance fighters of occupied Europe who used violence against their Nazi oppressors, because we accepted that their cause was just and their methods disciplined. Christians who refused to condemn the use of violence in an attempt to end injustice constantly needed to make such distinctions. They had to recognize that we had no right to condemn the use of violence by others in pursuit of justice if they were prepared to use it themselves for the same end. They should also acknowledge that down the ages there have been Christians to whom violence was morally repugnant but who had nevertheless resorted to it in an attempt to end a still greater evil. One of the best-known recent examples was Dietrich Bonhoeffer's participation in the plot to kill Hitler.

In the paper, we refuted as fraudulent the comparison by the Vorster government of black resistance in South Africa with terrorism in Europe. Instead we asked for a recognition of the rebellion in the country against the regime, and we quoted the black South African who lived through the June 1976 Soweto uprising: "I was in Soweto when the police came in. I saw them shoot an eight-year old child dead in the street. And you ask me to be non-violent?" Three effective ways for action were recommended in the paper: providing support to refugees, building support for those working for liberation inside South Africa, and working to end all foreign support to South Africa as demanded by black South Africans themselves.

The background paper was well received and considered useful in many churches and ecumenical groups. But the West German council of churches (EKD) reacted furiously. They argued that the "Sjollema Papier" (I had signed the covering letter) asked to legitimize violence by the black people of South Africa. This was going beyond the official WCC position as defined in Addis Ababa in 1971. The fact that we had headed one of the chapters "A just struggle" was considered by the EKD as particularly provoking. In the eyes of the EKD, the WCC had broken a taboo. A discussion about a just rebellion was, in their eyes, out of the question. What was the status of the paper? Was the WCC now asking for acceptance of a "just rebellion" as opposed to the "just-war" theology defended by many of the historical churches (including the Lutheran churches) in the past? The West German churches considered this unacceptable, especially in view of the recent Nazi era and Germany's extreme violence through the Shoah. Our initiative was considered irresponsible.

Had the EKD read the covering letter to our background paper more carefully, there would have been no reason for their reaction. But the notion of "background paper" (study paper), which the WCC had used regularly to feed an ecumenical discussion on specific issues, was apparently unknown in Germany and thus it seemed to them that we had transgressed our mandate. In an already tense situation between the EKD and "Geneva," this was the last straw.[23] In hindsight I must confess that we should have been more careful in using terms like "just rebellion": we might have avoided such a heated debate. But we needed to raise the issue one way or another, especially in light of misusing the theological and biblical concept "obedience" to the state (see Rom. 13). As the Kairos document would later state, this text has been often used to justify the interests of the state instead of it acting as "the servant of God" (Rom. 13:16).

An interesting comment on our paper came from Helmut Goll-witzer: he said that we should not have spoken about a just rebellion as this would imply that we recognized the South African government. Since the black majority in South Africa had no democratic rights, one could not consider the white minority regime as a legitimate government. He also criticized the EKD for demanding non-violence from the black people while refusing to deal with the violence of the white oppressors. Another commentator, James Forest, secretary of the International Fellowship of Reconciliation (IFOR), wrote that he disagreed about promoting a just rebellion because the black majority was helpless in the face of a powerful army which even possessed nuclear weapons. Even at this stage, he insisted, non-violent forms of resistance were possible and could be successful. Forest was right, as the following years would make clear when black groups all over South Africa helped to make the country more and more ungovernable.

The Dutch PCR support group Prepaid Reply reacted by saying that one should never use the term "just" in case of war or rebellion. Only history could (later on) consider whether a war or rebellion had been just. Moreover, in its 1971 Addis Ababa central committee resolution, the WCC had left open the possibility for the oppressed to redress their grievances through violent methods of resistance.

Combating racism throughout the WCC

Earlier I mentioned the problem of internal staff relations within PCR. But there were also frictions over PCR policies within the wider WCC staff and programmes. Gene Blake and especially Philip Potter emphasized time and again that combating racism was not only the work of a small sub-unit in the WCC. Rather the whole council and its entire staff, through their respective programmes – Faith and Order, Mission and Evangelism, Inter-Church Aid, Laity, the Women's Desk, the Youth Department, the Finance and Personnel Departments, the Bossey Ecumenical Institute, Bible Studies, Dialogue with Other Faiths, Education, etc. – needed to make clear our *joint ecumenical vision* of integrating unity, service, mission, and renewal. Each in its own field was to make its own contribution.

To this effect, a staff coordinating group was set up, chaired by Potter himself. Its discussions sometimes turned out to be difficult. Potter and we as PCR staff were time and again confronted with the rigidity and (sometimes understandable) self-interest of our colleagues in other parts of the WCC. They were afraid of "losing their time" with issues they considered outside their domain. They had difficulty in accepting their share in combating racism and in seeing this as an integral part of the WCC and thus of evident importance to their own work and that of the council as a whole.

That resistance came particularly, but not only, from the department of Faith and Order. At the 1969 Canterbury central committee, Lukas Vischer, its director, had in private questioned the growing militancy of the WCC in social inter-racial and international matters, as it would affect it as a fellowship of churches. He was in favour of developing a theology of racial justice *prior* to any action programmes. However, this was not in line with the thinking of the general secretary (supported by central committee) or the PCR itself. We could not wait any longer for action. Theological reflections on racism and racial justice would be developed and insights gained along the road, en route. Apart from personalities, it sometimes seemed that the old tensions between the autonomous Life and Work and Faith and Order movements were in play again. We in the PCR felt that Faith and Order produced too much "theoretical theology" and was too Western-oriented, while we were more in the line of contextual and liberation theology. Nevertheless, thanks to the support and insights of our Faith and Order colleague Geiko Müller-Fahenholz, his commission and the PCR (José Chipenda) jointly sponsored a consultation on "Racism in Theology and Theology against Racism," which attempted to respond to a 1974 central committee request for further reflection (including theological) on problems connected with the struggle against racism.

In his report as WCC general secretary to the 1983 WCC Vancouver assembly, Potter was forced to ask whether the WCC could continue "to go its own way with programmes and activities reaching to groups and others, but not conceived, planned, communicated at all stages, and carried out with the active involvement of the churches."[24] It had become clear that a gap was developing between the WCC and the hierarchy of the member churches. In fact, it became a crisis in the ecumenical fellowship. Through its different networks, the WCC's links with local congregations and with ecumenical and secular groups had simultaneously been strengthened. The radical policies and projects developed by the PCR had certainly contributed to the crisis, yet these policies were the result of what the delegates at the 1968 Uppsala assembly had clearly asked for. So it appeared that the member churches were after all not willing to follow the road they had themselves chosen. And in taking this stance, they unfortunately followed the general worldwide political and economic conservative trend of the moment.

In the WCC there was a growing consciousness about the theological justification of revolutionary violence. The issue received increasing attention as the churches were confronted with liberation struggles in many parts of the world. The 1966 world conference on Church and Society raised the question "whether the violence which sheds blood in planned revolutions may not be a lesser evil than the violence which, though bloodless, condemns whole populations to perennial despair."[25] At the request of the central committee, the WCC's department on Church and Society produced a study on these moral dilemmas, "Violence, Non-violence and the Struggle for Social Justice" (the Martin Luther King resolution), which stressed that the goal of revolutionary action was not the destruction of the enemy but a more just social order. It distinguished three different points of view on the use of force in resisting oppression: those believing exclusively in non-violence; those accepting violence only in extreme circumstances; and those believing that violence is unavoidable in certain situations. The report also underlined that non-violent action can be highly political and controversial. David Gill, the author, later wrote, "Both pacifism and the just-war theory are feeling their inadequacies in the developing ecumenical debates about militarism, weapons of mass destruction and revolutionary conflict."[26] Furthermore, one should remember that when churches were horrified at violence, the issue was not always between non-violence and violence, but between engagement and non-engagement in the struggle for justice. It was change that people feared.[27]

The sub-unit on Women in Church and Society, under the leadership of Brigalia Bam and later of Bärbel von Wartenberg, quickly understood the need for combating racism alongside the struggle against sexism and discrimination against women: they were interrelated.

Hans-Ruedi Weber, responsible for WCC biblical studies, in a paper on "Prophecy in the Ecumenical Movement," commented,

> This Programme to Combat Racism was not only a response to a clear prophetic challenge, but it has itself become a prophetic action with all the characteristic dangers, ambiguities and divisive

effects of prophecy. No wonder that it was in this connection that the prophetic vocation of the church became a subject for theological reflection in the ecumenical movement ... Through its Programme to Combat Racism the World Council of Churches has in a large unplanned way and to its own astonishment stumbled into the role of a partly acclaimed and often hated prophet. Yet to the vocation of an ecumenical agent belongs also very centrally the ministry of reconciliation... Many thoughtful Christians all over the world begin to wonder whether through its Programme to Combat Racism the World Council of Churches is in fact a true or a false prophet. What begins as true prophecy can develop into false prophecy. The churches therefore desperately need criteria for discerning a true or a false prophet.[28]

The division of World Mission and Evangelism cooperated by organizing meetings with different mission agencies on race issues in their work in particular countries, such as Zimbabwe, Angola, and Mozambique. These meetings made it possible to hear how the missions in the field felt about PCR's involvement in that region. At the same time, we could fill them in on what our policies were. This also gave us the possibility to consult them about future PCR projects that touched on their territory. Nevertheless, it must be said that there was quite a bit of anxiety on the part of the Swiss and German missions working in Mozambique and Namibia, as they were concerned about the safety of their personnel.

The contribution of the Commission on the Churches' Participation in Development (CCPD) was centred on the issue of growing power of "recipient groups" and a people-centred approach. The education desk's major contribution was through Paolo Freire's *Pedagogy of the Oppressed*, published in English in 1970.[29] Central to Freire's thinking was the idea of "conscientization," the conviction that the poor should have the right to analyze their own society and become subjects of their own destiny. The Bossey Ecumenical Institute became involved in the WCC's overall anti-racism policy by providing additional scholarships to students from Southern Africa, some of whom lived in exile.

But perhaps most directly involved was the Communication department, which on an almost daily basis had to cope with the media reporting on WCC/PCR policies and the different reactions this provoked in the churches as well as the media. This meant radio broadcasting, TV, and articles and interviews in the secular and religious press in different languages. Cooperation between PCR and Communication was very important but not always easy, as the Communication staff sought to maintain good relations with the media, including those that were most critical of us.

One particular test came when the president of the Federal Republic of Germany, Gustav Heinemann, came to the WCC in 1976 in the context of a state visit to Switzerland. In view of the continuing critical attitude of the West German churches, I saw a chance to improve PCR's image in that country. At the advice of Bé Ruys of the Hendrik Kraemer Haus in Berlin, I contacted the well-known German theologian Helmut Gollwitzer. He was a good friend of Heinemann: both had played a role in the German confessing church during the Second World War. I asked Gollwitzer whether he would be willing to suggest to Heinemann that he make a positive reference to the PCR and its Special Fund in the speech he would deliver at the WCC. This would no doubt have an effect on the West German EKD and the regional churches it grouped. Gollwitzer said he would try, but made clear the overwhelming administrative and political sensitivities within the German presidency.

I had not said anything to anyone about this initiative except to my direct colleagues in PCR. The arrangement with the German presidency was that one day before his arrival in Geneva, Heinemann's speech to the WCC would be transmitted from Bern to the WCC Communication department for translation into English and French. But its German director, Jürgen Hilke, was reluctant to share the content of the speech with the PCR. So I had to make a deal with one of his associates. When the speech arrived I saw that there was no reference to PCR. I made a last attempt by phoning Gollwitzer, who after some hesitation agreed to phone the president's press secretary. Finally, one hour before Heinemann's arrival, I received an excited phone call from the Communication department, saying that there was a last minute addition to Heinemann's speech and that there was special reference to the PCR! I was of course delighted. As he left the hall after Heinemann's speech, Visser 't Hooft came up to me and whispered with a grin, "Well done" – I don't know who told him. Perhaps he suspected a little plot on our part!

At one point I gave a press conference in London, arranged by the British Council of Churches. There were quite a few journalists and plenty of questions. My introduction indicated the need to intensify the isolation of the Pretoria regime in answer to its growing violence against anyone opposing apartheid inside the country. The daily *Guardian* afterwards reported extensively on what I had said, but entirely misinterpreted my introduction, suggesting I had spoken in terms of further impoverishing the black people so that they would revolt openly against the regime. As a result, Philip Potter received a furious message from John Rees, general secretary of the SACC, protesting about my statement: he understood that the consequence of what I had said would make the black population of South Africa suffer even more. On return to Geneva, Potter asked me for an explanation. I gave him the text of my statement, which satisfied him and which he sent to Rees.

On a personal note

All of us in the PCR were often under considerable pressure. In 1978, after eight years, I was suffering from burn-out and asked for sick leave. It took me nearly six weeks to recover, during which time I had to dose myself with sleeping pills – not the ideal solution, of course. José Chipenda would come to see me and fill me in on latest developments. And Gisela Gregoriades would in urgent situations phone me at home. But on the whole, my colleagues respected my need to rest.

At home I had tried over the years to keep my wife and children abreast of the most essential developments in the PCR, although there were not many opportunities to do so. But Jet had her own preoccupations with the running of the household and looking after our four children (at that time between 14 and 22 years old), and she bore the brunt of my frequent absences. Sometimes I would invite visitors or colleagues home for dinner who would tell their stories. But overall my hope and wish to have Jet involved in the race issue proved impossible. Coming home late from the office or from travel, it was not always easy to adjust. And Jet and the children would sometimes resent it when I tended to take things in hand. The Uppsala dream proved difficult to realize at home. My family simply lived in a different world from mine, and this demanded a fair amount of patience and adjustment from us all. I was therefore extremely grateful for all the support Jet gave me: without her understanding and encouragement I would never have been able to continue for the nearly twelve years I spent in the PCR.

After a holiday away from Geneva and relaxing walks in the mountains, I returned to the office ready to face the last period of two years with the PCR, before I left for the International Labour Office to become responsible for its anti-apartheid programme.

1. Visit of Dr Peter Heyde and the author to Ecumenical Patriarch Athenagoras I in Constantinople in 1962 to discuss ecumenical support for Greek Orthodox migrants in Western Europe. *Photo by B. Sjollema.*

2. The American author James Baldwin addressing the WCC's Uppsala assembly in 1968. His contribution was vital for the creation of the WCC's Programme to Combat Racism one year later. *Photo by John Taylor, WCC.*

3. From left to right: Rev. Nicolas Maro, secretary of the Christian Council of Tanzania; Rev. Uria Simango, vice president of Frelimo; and Eduardo Mondlane, president of Frelimo – after Mondlane accepted to be the keynote speaker at the WCC consultation that prepared the creation of the Programme to Combat Racism. Three days later, on 3 February 1969, Mondlane was assassinated by a parcel bomb. *Photo by B. Sjollema.*

4. The head table during the 1969 WCC Notting Hill consultation on racism, which proposed the mandate for PCR. From left to right: Rena Karefa Smart, WCC staff; US Senator George McGovern, moderator of the consultation; Eugene Carson Blake, WCC general secretary; the author; and Jean Fairfax, member of the WCC central committee. *Photo by John Taylor, WCC.*

5. The group that drafted the criteria of the Special Fund to Combat Racism in July 1970 at the Limuru conference centre near Nairobi. From left to right: Rev. In Ha Lee (Korea/Japan); Rev. José Chipenda (Angola); Dag Dawood (Sri Lanka); Rev. Gonzalo Castillo-Cardenas (Colombia); Pauline Webb (UK); the author; Joyce Clague (Australia). *Photo by Pauline Webb.*

6. PCR's three executive staff members at the 1972 central committee meeting of the WCC in Utrecht (Netherlands). From left to right: Rev. Charles Spivey (US); Dag Dawood (Sri Lanka); and the author. *Photo by WCC.*

7. In 1976, Rev. Rein Jan van der Veen donating, on behalf of the Dutch support group for PCR, a cheque for 60,000 Dutch guilders to WCC General Secretary Philip Potter and Central Committee Moderator Archbishop Edward Scott, for the Special Fund to Combat Racism. *Photo by John Taylor, WCC.*

8. The author with acting ANC president, Oliver R. Tambo, after the latter addressed the 1986 Annual Labour Conference of the ILO. *Photo by ILO.*

9. Nelson Mandela visiting the WCC soon after his liberation in 1990 to thank the council and its member churches personally for the support they had given to the struggle against apartheid. Next to him is his wife, Winnie Mandela. *Photo by Peter Williams, WCC.*

10. Long queues of voters, black and white, on election day in April 1994. *Photo by B. Sjollema.*

11. In 1994: Former president of Zambia Kenneth Kaunda, leader of the Ecumenical Monitoring Programme in South Africa, together with the author after the results of the first democratic elections were announced, *Photo by B. Sjollema*

12. The author and his wife, Jet, after he received the Order of the Companions of Oliver R. Tambo in Pretoria, 2004. *Photo by B. Sjollema,*

13. The author receiving the Order of the Companions of Oliver R. Tambo from South African President Thabo Mbeki in 2004. *Photo by Henriette Sjollema.*

8. Support and Criticism

Meanwhile, the discussions on PCR's policies in the member churches continued unabated. In fact, the questions the churches raised often went far beyond the issue of race, and concerned rather the whole of the WCC in its struggle for justice and peace as part of its understanding of ecumenism. But because of its visibility and the sensitive issues it raised, the PCR often became the symbol of what the WCC as a whole stood for.

Heated debates included not only the question of violence by oppressors and counter-violence by the oppressed, but also the central and long-standing issue of racism within and reconciliation between churches. For instance, churches in the Netherlands, Germany, and Switzerland had century-long relations with the white racist Afrikaner churches in South Africa, and their policy had been "dialogue" with the white churches to avoid breaking off relations. But endless discussions had not resulted in any progress or change of mind among the Afrikaners. Now, from an ecumenical point of view, the issue had become how to act in solidarity with the black people and their movement for liberation.

Much of the reluctance on the part of the Western churches had to do with these historical links with the white churches and a lack of understanding of post-colonial developments. To them, solidarity meant primarily support for the white establishment. And this was precisely what the WCC and the PCR were calling into question. Ecumenical theology pointed increasingly away from reconciliation as a problem between people and highlighted instead the structural problem: How to achieve justice for peoples, and how to express real solidarity with the victims of oppression instead of giving paternalistic advice.

Racism was undermining reconciliation, and a different relationship with the victims of racism became the centre of the debate. South Africa was no longer seen as a white nation with a black problem, but as a black nation under white oppression.[1] We needed to analyze the situation anew from the perspective of the black people. Contacts with black leaders, their churches, and the resistance movements became a priority. Many churches in the West were insufficiently aware of these movements and their goals and needed to be informed about them.

Equally important were the consequences of this shift in emphasis. Solidarity with the oppressed meant disinvestment from the multinational corporations benefiting from the exploitation of black workers and closing accounts with banks making loans to the apartheid regime. This was totally new thinking for many Christians and churches in Europe and it created tensions at many church levels.

But most importantly, the challenge for a radical change in the thinking of the white Western churches came from South African Christians themselves. First, there were strong statements by individual Christian leaders, in particular Beyers Naudé, Wolfram Kistner, Allan Boesak, Frank Chikane, and Desmond Tutu. Then the South African Council of Churches (SACC) began to take the lead by confronting the so-called Christian white minority government in Pretoria with the demands of the gospel and demanding justice for the black majority instead of oppression.

In 1982, the Dutch Reformed Mission Church, under the leadership of Allan Boesak, drafted its courageous Belhar Confession. It was an "outcry of faith" and a "call for faithfulness and repentance," and confronted the Reformed churches with the sin of racism. The confession aimed to help bring about reconciliation between these churches and thus contribute to reconciliation within the nation of

South Africa. In that same year, the general assembly of the World Alliance of Reformed Churches (WARC), following a similar decision by the Lutheran World Federation (LWF) in Dar-es-Salaam in 1977, decided that the apartheid situation in South African represented a *status confessionis,* a situation on which the church had to take a stand. Apartheid was unequivocally rejected as a heresy. Because the responses of the white Lutheran church and two white Reformed churches in South Africa were unsatisfactory, both world bodies declared the suspension of these churches. These were extraordinary decisions. They clearly indicated that the churches worldwide could not be neutral. Past and present, they had been "drifting away from the poor and powerless to the rich and mighty,"[2] but they had to take sides with the oppressed. It was the beginning of a long learning process.

Beyers Naudé: An extraordinary witness

At this point, I want to make special mention of Beyers Naudé, as someone who stands out in making me aware of the history of apartheid and the role of the churches both in supporting and opposing it. And if there is one person among the white people of South Africa who represented for me the conscience of the apartheid nation and the need for costly discipleship, it is again Beyers.

Just after the first grants to liberation movement were made, he was on a tour in West Germany to explain to the churches the latest developments in South Africa. But at each meeting he was of course asked about his opinion of the Special Fund grants. This embarrassed him because he himself was not yet convinced about the justification of the WCC's decision. As he explained to us, he was afraid of possible repercussions for the black opposition inside the country. Yet he understood that the situation in South Africa had deteriorated to such an extent that the WCC's move had become unavoidable.

As director of the Christian Institute he was constantly moving around in and outside South Africa, and he would listen carefully to the many questions people raised. Often church leaders in Holland, Britain, and West Germany drew him into discussions to see if he could be quoted as someone from inside the country who was opposed to the WCC move, whereas in South Africa the government accused him of support for violence and contacts with the liberation movements.

After the Christian Institute was banned in 1977, Beyers and Wolfram Kistner created the Ecumenical Advice Bureau in Johannesburg in 1988. Kistner's presence and his considerable theological and historical input were of enormous support to Beyers. In addition, his quiet voice, his gentleness, and his endless patience were essential in helping Beyers weather the storm as the apartheid crisis came to a head. Kistner had been director of the division of justice and reconciliation of the SACC from 1976 to 1988, when Beyers was its caretaker general secretary.

In spite of deep roots in the Afrikaner community, Beyers was able to identify with the aspirations of the black people of his country. He gradually accepted the importance of black theology and the black consciousness movement, which in his opinion were the best way to tackle injustice in South Africa. For this he suffered rejection by his own people, the Afrikaners, as well as a banning order for seven years. He said, "I am crying for my Afrikaner people. I am trying to say to them that they will never have a future unless they are prepared to live with others."[3] That is exactly what Beyers, a humble man, tried to do. The prophetic voices of both Naudé and Kistner will be with us for a long time.

Support for the PCR

Without the continuing strong support of the WCC central and executive committees, the PCR would not have been able to carry on with its programme of action over the years. But that support could not be taken for granted. Because of the high profile of the PCR's activities, we had to prepare carefully for these committee meetings, knowing that their members, and the churches they represented, were often under considerable pressure from conservative groups and the media back home.

Support came from a limited number of member churches, and more often from national and regional councils of churches. But significantly, we gradually received considerable assistance from many radical local ecumenical and church support groups, which organized themselves specifically to defend the PCR in order to correct the erroneous impression that their church leaders automatically represented their views. These groups were made up mostly of young people who were enthusiastic about the PCR's initiatives, which they saw as an example of what the church needed to be doing. In West Germany, several ecumenical groups (notably Pro Ökumene, Ökumenisches Forum, Solidarische Kirche, Mainzer Arbeitskreis Südliches Afrika, Evangelische Frauenarbeit in Deutschland, and the Plädoyer für eine Ökumenische Zukunft) were concerned about the growing distance between the Evangelical Church in Germany (EKD) and the WCC. They wanted to correct the negative image their church leaders were giving of the WCC, and the PCR in particular. These groups developed direct links with the WCC and the PCR, independent of the church bureaucracy, which in the German situation was very hierarchical. The Plädoyer group became especially important: originally created (1979) in support of the PCR, it became the conscience of the EKD, reminding it of its ecumenical responsibilities and warning it of the danger of isolating itself from the worldwide ecumenical family. For the PCR, these different groups became valuable partners in finding approaches to the conservative German situation and involving the official churches more in combating racism.

The issue of violence appeared to be the most difficult problem for the German churches. While violence by the state was acceptable, it was often defined as terrorism when used by racially oppressed people. The Plädoyer group, together with other ecumenical groups, stated that it was hypocritical to demand that the powerless use only non-violent resistance. Plädoyer also called on the German churches to develop their own programme to combat racism, stating that combating racism worldwide is only credible when we do the same at home. In spite of strong pressure by the EKD, German church women (Evangelische Frauenarbeit in Deutschland-EFD) organized a very successful campaign called "Don't buy the fruits of apartheid," involving women both inside and outside the churches. This most welcome support by the younger generation of Christians in West Germany gave us hope and showed that the ecumenical movement was alive and well, in spite of the discouraging resistance and even hostility on the part of the EKD toward our work.

In East Germany, thanks in particular to our PCR commission member Elisabeth Adler, the Bund der Evangelische Kirchen (council of churches) fully supported the PCR, but had to ask itself why it was regularly congratulated by government officials.

It was evident that political issues and tensions between East and West Germany played an important role in the attitude of the East German government. Eastern socialist countries saw the PCR as an anti-capitalist element in the WCC that they would tacitly approve of. This did not help us in our relations with the EKD, of course. When the German edition of Adler's assessment of the first five years of the PCR was published by the council of churches in East Germany, the EKD was displeased and decided to print a West German edition with its own introduction!

The Dutch royal family, as members of the Netherlands Reformed Church, had from the beginning shown considerable interest in the ecumenical movement. After hearing about the Special Fund and support to liberation movements, Queen Juliana invited Prepaid Reply chairperson Rein Jan van der Veen, Henk Berkhof (a member of the WCC central committee), and myself in 1971 to explain to her the objectives of the PCR and the fund. She was well informed, and questioned the aims and purposes of the fund and asked how this related to reconciliation and peace between black and white people. After a lively two-hour discussion, she seemed satisfied with the answers. A few weeks after our visit she made a personal donation to the fund, which created headlines in the Dutch and foreign media. For us in the PCR, this was a real feather in our cap, and the queen's gesture led many other people inside and outside the churches to follow suit.

Because of Holland's close cultural and family ties with the white South African minority, discussions about the PCR in that country were sensitive. For centuries the Dutch had emigrated to South Africa. There were long-standing relations between the Reformed churches in the Netherlands and the white Dutch Reformed churches in South Africa. Thus, in the beginning the churches were hesitant to act and had to be pushed by ecumenical action groups, like Kairos and particularly Prepaid Reply.

Kairos' main objective was to support the Christian Institute of South Africa. It stimulated better relations with the black churches in South Africa and launched an anti-emigration campaign to the country. Prepaid Reply took strong action in support of the PCR from the beginning. It was very successful in fund-raising for the Special Fund, and it was also involved in implementing the WCC resolutions on banking and disinvestment through active participation in shareholder meetings of key Dutch multinationals like Shell, Philips and Unilever. In addition, it organized meetings with the leaders of these and other multinationals, as well as with several banks, including ABN and AMRO. This greatly stimulated the synods of a number of churches to follow suit. Prepaid Reply had a policy of regularly involving the media in order to stimulate debate beyond the churches. The Netherlands Reformed Church and the Reformed Churches in the Netherlands adopted a step-by-step approach, but on the disinvestment issue they could not decide between a "reform approach" and an outright call for withdrawal. The council of churches, on the other hand, accepted a withdrawal strategy in support of the oppressed black majority. The Dutch government showed its support for the PCR by making several sizable contributions to the Special Fund. The Dutch anti-apartheid movement played a key role in alerting public opinion and put pressure on political parties and trade unions.

For me personally, the support we received from the Dutch was absolutely essential. Holland was after all still my base and it would have been disastrous if I had been left isolated. But in fact I had calls from friends, supporters, and the media almost daily, and especially from our PCR commission member and friend Rein Jan van der Veen, comforting us with positive news about churches and ecumenical groups taking more radical positions in our support. And most important, when there was a crisis in Holland, he would see to it that things would be straightened out. Van der Veen and Pauline Webb in Britain were the most trustworthy and committed committee members on whom I could always rely. And that made all the difference!

In Great Britain, the supporters of the PCR pleaded the cause of disinvestment with the finance committees of the major churches (including the church commissioners of the Church of England) and the British Council of Churches (BCC). At the initiative of David Haslam they started the campaign "End Loans to South Africa." The PCR's naming of corporations directly investing in or trading with Southern Africa put pressure on all the BCC's member churches to check their portfolios. The discussion this engendered within the churches on the whole subject of investment ethics led eventually in Britain to the creation of EIRIS, the Ethical Investment Research and Information Service.

Pauline Webb writes in her memoirs:

> I learned through all these debates what an eloquent symbol money has become ... [O]n the one hand people complained bitterly about our making funds available to meet the humanitarian needs of the oppressed struggling to make their voices heard in the world, while on the other hand the same people found it unacceptable that money should be withdrawn from businesses and banks profiting from exploitative and discriminatory practices. When we launched the Special Fund we had said that we needed an action that would speak louder than any words. It certainly seemed that by "putting our money where our mouth was" people did hear the message we were trying to convey.[4]

Criticisms of the WCC

Inevitably there was criticism from certain member churches, but also from within the staff, some of whom questioned the wisdom of our actions. Many colleagues were understandably resentful that wherever they went to speak about their own programmes and projects, they were always asked questions about the PCR. Not only were they forced to spend more time explaining and defending our programme than talking about their own concerns, but they always had to carry PCR material with them. So there were often lively discussions before or after they had been travelling. From our point of view in the PCR, however, this reinforced our understanding that a programme to combat racism had to be carried by the whole WCC and not just by a few PCR staff members.

Although Visser 't Hooft was in favour of the WCC further developing its activities in the field of social and economic justice, in private he questioned the decision to take action as directly as it did through the PCR and its Special Fund. And because a number of member churches (especially in Germany and Switzerland) were critical of the PCR, they tried to induce him to voice his criticism openly. But his loyalty to the WCC prevailed and he avoided taking such a position publicly.

While I never asked Visser 't Hooft what his objections were, it is probably correct to say that he felt the WCC's role should be limited to supporting its member churches and encouraging them to take the necessary action each in their own context. Perhaps he followed ecumenical pioneer J. H. Oldham's thinking, expressed as early as the 1937 Oxford world conference on church, community, and state: he felt that the WCC's role was not to undertake large studies but to encourage its member churches to do so in their own context. However, we should remember that the WCC's single most visible and concrete action – even before it was officially created – had been its service to refugees, which started already during the Second World War. It was the churches themselves that specifically mandated the WCC to act, both in the case of refugees and now in the crisis situation of worldwide racism.

As to the WCC member churches, they were clearly often negatively influenced by the secular media, and critical voices frequently reflected or even repeated what had been stated in the press. Conservatives in some member churches in Western Europe, in particular in Britain, Germany, and Switzerland, complained about the fact that the WCC had moved from its original, largely Western, concept of political responsibility to a more radical ideology and the theology of liberation. Thus, the WCC's decision to make grants to liberation movements in Southern Africa – which used largely non-violent, but sometimes violent, methods of change – caused serious dissension in some influential churches.

This decision was probably one of the most controversial in the WCC's history. The ecumenical fellowship did not break, but the Presbyterian Church of Ireland withdrew from the WCC, while the Evangelical Lutheran Church of Schaumburg-Lippe, the smallest of the provincial churches in the EKD, suspended its membership. The Salvation Army first suspended its membership and later accepted fraternal status with the WCC as a Christian world communion.

Some churches also criticized the PCR's "one-sided" concentration on Southern Africa. Why so much emphasis on apartheid and colonialism in Southern Africa, and so little on racism and human rights in Eastern Europe? Why were we so tough on colonial rule and apartheid in South Africa, and so soft on communist tyranny in Eastern Europe? Racism in the Soviet Union, Eastern Europe, or even China was overlooked, they argued. These accusations were no doubt politically motivated and had to be seen to be made. It must be remembered that we were still living in the era of the Cold War and our actions were scrutinized by the media, politicians and church leaders alike.

In Britain, a member of the House of Lords, Lord Sudeley, collected information about me personally. In a letter of 30 November 1974, he wrote to a staff member of the Dutch Inter-University Institute for Missiology and Ecumenical Affairs, speculating that "the history of Dr Sjollema might suggest that he has or has had communist affiliations." Revealingly, though, he went on to say,

Now I am accumulating material for a debate which Lord Arran has indicated that he would at one point like to bring before the House of Lords on Christian unity. The main purpose of my speech for his debate would be to attack the World Council of Churches for promoting the Programme to Combat Racism as a movement which, it may be suspected, is instigated by communists who aim particularly at raw materials and the Cape route of South Africa. The difficulty I have experienced in building up such a speech, however, is to get together enough hard facts to back up my general supposition, and I am hoping so much you will not take it amiss that I should appeal to yourself for information.[5]

It is perfectly correct to say that PCR focused primarily on areas mainly in the Western hemisphere. This was because of the clear mandate we were given to deal especially with *white racism*. Combating white racism was in itself already more than we could cope with. Also, given the small budget at our disposal and the few staff we were, we could not possibly take on the whole world! Critics of our one-sidedness also overlooked the fact that the PCR developed sizeable programmes in support of racially oppressed groups in many other parts of the world: for instance, Indigenous peoples such as the Aborigines in Australia, the Maoris in New Zealand, the Inuit in Canada, Indians in the US, as well as many different Indian peasant groups in Latin America. But their cause hardly made front-page news.

The WCC's enemies

Vehement criticism came from two long-standing enemies of the WCC.

In 1979 the ultra-conservative American Ernest W. Lefever published *Amsterdam to Nairobi: The World Council of Churches and the Third World*,[6] strongly criticizing the WCC's social thinking. Several South African embassies in Europe distributed the German edition of Lefever's book free of charge to local pastors and congregations as well as to the media, with an accompanying letter. The book was highly praised by the conservative American commentator George F. Will, whose columns were widely published in newspapers.

Lefever was at one time a pacifist and a minister in the Church of the Brethren in the US. In 1976 he launched the Ethics and Public Policy Center, a right-wing think-tank that at one point received funding from Nestlé, among others. Later he was appointed assistant secretary of state for human rights under the Reagan administration, but failed to win confirmation by Congress. Sixty organizations, among them the national council of churches, had formed an ad hoc committee to oppose his congressional approval.

Lefever was a strong anti-communist. His criticism of the WCC was concentrated on the policies and programmes of the PCR and the WCC's alleged acceptance of liberation theology, which, he said, was "in its manifestation and vocabulary ... virtually indistinguishable from a Marxist-Leninist world-view."[7] In particular, he found the 1978 grant to the Zimbabwe Patriotic Front objectionable because the Front "believes in deliberately murdering missionaries and their families; ... shoot[s] down unarmed civilian planes; and is motivated by a Marxist and racist vision of society."[8] Nowhere did Lefever mention the behaviour of the Ian Smith regime and its white racist policies. Because of its natural resources and strategic location, he said, South Africa ought to be a "close ally" of the US and a "full-fledged partner in the struggle against communist expansion."[9] Repeatedly he suggested that non-democratic, non-Western or non-Anglo-Saxon peoples were insensitive to human rights as Americans understood them, and were incapable of self-government.

Lefever's book was critically reviewed by John C. Bennett in *Christianity and Crisis*,[10] and by my WCC colleague Paul Abrecht in *The Christian Century*,[11] who observed that the attention given to these writings in neo-conservative circles, especially in the US, raised serious questions about their integrity. Lefever had written a simplistic, biased, and essentially confused and contradictory account of the social thought and action of the WCC. The book drew wide attention elsewhere as well. Lefever also commented on Martin Luther King's famous speech at Riverside Drive church in April 1967, criticizing him for his unfactual and unfair attack on the United States when King linked the civil-rights movement with the opposition to the Vietnam war and subtly praised the communist and revolutionary forces of "liberation." In an article in the *Wall Street Journal* (21 May 1980) Lefever wrote that "some WCC leaders also find Marxist views attractive because they hope to recapture moral authority in an increasingly complex and secular world by running with the radical-chic pack."

Later, the WCC also came under concerted attack in the US in a series of articles in *The Reader's Digest,* and a CBS television documentary. WCC staff and American members of the WCC central committee tried hard to correct this false image of the WCC and the PCR, but they found it extremely difficult to get their reactions printed. These attempts to clarify the WCC's policies and programmes were important. Though at times such attacks put the WCC on the defensive, they created many occasions to state positively what its objectives were and why the situation was so urgent. Racism was destroying humanity in its search for a fellowship of men and women living together in justice and peace.

Ironically, one point that was overlooked in the struggle with our opponents about our support to the liberation movement, which they labelled pro-communist, was that this support had in fact tended to reduce these movements' dependence on communist services and encouraged their autonomy and more openness to other relationships.

But our real enemies were in the South African government, which was heavily involved in a smear campaign against the WCC. Several organizations – like the Christian League of Southern Africa, the Rhodesia Christian Group, the Christian Affirmation League, the International Christian Network, the Club of Ten, the International Society for Human Rights, and others – attacked the SACC and the WCC. Less known was the extent to which the South African government was directly or indirectly actually involved in several of these and other organizations and projects. Its aim was clearly to influence church affairs inside and outside South Africa. The methods used included personal contacts by inviting church leaders to visit South Africa, financial aid, conferences, advertisements, and publications. The Christian League grew and was thought to have strong financial government backing, although it refused to reveal its sources of support.

Prime minister John Vorster had originally denied all knowledge of these smear campaigns, but under increasing pressure in parliament and in the media, in 1978 he admitted that he had known about the secret funding to "assist in a delicate and unconventional way in combating the total onslaught of propaganda against South Africa" since 1972. Connie Mulder, the South African minister of information, approved a plan to improve South Africa's standing abroad by funding secret projects outside the country through the defence budget. The disclosure of this secret funding, called the "Muldergate" scandal, ruined the careers of a number of government employees. It became clear that the target of these smear campaigns were primarily the churches in South Africa and the WCC.

The subsequent exposure of a South African spy, Craig Williamson (a South African officer in the secret service) working in the International University Exchange Fund (IUEF) in Geneva made things worse. He was appointed deputy director of the IUEF and became responsible for the desk granting scholarships to South African students who wanted to study abroad. He was thus in a unique position to gather detailed information about all the applicants, many of whom were related to clandestine liberation movements. After several years in Geneva, he went back to South African with all the material he had gathered. As a result, dozens of South African applicants were arrested and tortured. Williamson tried to make contacts with other non-governmental agencies in Geneva, including the WCC. I met him several times at NGO meetings but did not trust him from the start.

One example of the smear campaign against the WCC took the form of several full-page advertisements in the Dutch (Christian) newspaper *Trouw*, in which the Club of Ten attacked not only the WCC but also individual staff members. Thus, in *Trouw* Philip Potter and I were singled out as supporters of terrorists with blood on our hands. Fortunately we could count on our friends in the Netherlands, especially the PCR support group Prepaid Reply, which undertook to rectify the story publicly. Rein Jan van der Veen, chairperson of

Prepaid Reply, went out of his way to counter these false allegations by exposing the fact that the money for these ads did not come from concerned individuals but from a South African government agency. Several of the South African organizations had extreme right-wing connections in Western Europe and North America. They created the International Christian Network as an umbrella organization to oppose the WCC more effectively. Its chairman, Peter Beyerhaus, professor of mission and ecumenical studies in Tübingen, Germany, was a former missionary in South Africa and an outspoken critic of the WCC.

In addition, the South African Foundation, established in 1959, which claimed to be independent and financed by private enterprise, opened offices in Paris, London, Bonn, and Washington with the aim of maintaining investor confidence in South Africa. It regularly sponsored tours for key decision-makers in both industry and the churches. Church leaders from West Germany, in particular, but also from Switzerland accepted invitations by the Foundation.

The vicious attacks by so-called Christian groups against the WCC frightened some member churches. But it soon became clear that these were not the spontaneous protests they first appeared.

The response of churches

In view of the member churches' criticisms in particular, the 1979 WCC central committee in Kingston, Jamaica, at the recommendation of the general secretary Philip Potter, decided on a worldwide review of the policies and programmes of the PCR in order to verify whether it still had sufficient backing of its constituency. That year-long intensive process culminated in a world consultation at Noordwijkerhout, Netherlands, in 1980 on the theme "The Churches Responding to Racism in the 1980s." It recommended both confirming the emphasis on Southern Africa and strengthening certain other sectors of its programme, in particular the issue of land rights, which was at the heart of the struggle for survival of Indigenous peoples.

In 1981 – after I left the WCC – a WCC team went to Australia to express solidarity with the Aboriginals and to discuss with the Australian churches their responsibility to combat racism. The team's report caused considerable controversy, not least among political leaders in Australia, as it demanded drastic changes in government policies on Aboriginal affairs. This was valuable since it heightened the visibility of the Aboriginal organizations.

As a result of the team visit, the WCC central committee approved a statement on land rights, which included recognition of "racist beliefs which identify Indigenous people as being sub-human, and which refuse to acknowledge the very existence of their spiritual, cultural, social, political and legal systems." The committee also recommended member churches should "become politically involved on the side of the Indigenous peoples and join the struggle against those powers and principalities which seek to deny the land rights and human rights of Indigenous Peoples."[12]

In 1989 the PCR sponsored a global consultation on "Land Is Our Life" in Darwin, Australia. It called on the international community to "consider the connection between racism and the consequent historical denial of Indigenous rights, including land rights and the inherent right to self-determination." Most importantly, it invited the WCC to recognize that "Indigenous lands have been taken by the church, without the consent of the Indigenous people of that land."[13] Later, at the WCC's assembly in 1991 in Canberra, there was a significant representation of Aboriginal people. They had in fact been involved in the preparation of the assembly, and the tribe whose traditional land covered Canberra were the first to welcome the delegates. In 1995, a full-time Indigenous consultant joined the WCC staff and much emphasis was put on capacity-building within Indigenous nations in Latin America, Asia, Europe, and the Pacific. Indigenous spirituality and the land became a major issue.

An important new aspect of PCR's work after Canberra was casteism and the extremely grave situation of more than one hundred million Dalits in India, formerly known as untouchables but today recognized as the Indigenous Peoples of India. The PCR supported the establishment of the Dalit Solidarity Programme (which later became the Dalit Solidarity Peoples) which brought together for the first time in the history of India Dalits of Muslim, Hindu, Sikh, Buddhist, and Christian faith communities. The discrimination of Dalits in India was gradually recognized as being as serious a violation of human rights as was apartheid in South Africa.[14]

1981: Leaving the WCC

In 1981 I left the WCC after nearly 12 years in the PCR and altogether 25 years in the WCC's service. The 1979 central committee had decided that executive personnel should serve no more than nine years on the staff. This meant that a number of old-timers, like C. I. Itty, Brigalia Bam, Lukas Vischer and Leopoldo Niilus, as well as myself, had to leave. The idea behind this decision was to favour the hiring of staff from developing countries as well as more Orthodox, women, and youth. I understood and accepted the need for these changes, but I felt that the rigidity with which this policy was implemented meant that the WCC lost much of its sense of history and continuity. Newly appointed staff often had little or no ecumenical experience. The WCC tended to become a bureaucracy of the churches and to my mind lost much of its original sense of an ecumenical movement.

I had in these twelve years become "Mr PCR" – or at least I must confess I felt like this. I sometimes had the feeling that I was indispensable, and I should probably have realized that after eight or ten years, certainly in that kind of job, one should go. After a first period with a white European, there was a feeling that it was now time for a black director from South Africa.

My direct successor was Anwar Barkat, a member of the WCC executive committee. I had meanwhile accepted that I had to leave the WCC altogether, but I was very concerned about a successor who would be committed as I had been. Barkat was a political scientist from Pakistan who had found refuge in the US because of the political situation in his country. He wanted a job in the WCC and was strongly supported by some American members of the central committee.

Barkat served the PCR from 1981 until 1987. He was succeeded by Barney Pityana, a black Anglican priest from South Africa who brought new insights and broadened its scope. During the 1980s, the crisis in South Africa was rapidly coming to a climax. Many churches and especially the SACC concretely involved themselves in the struggle against apartheid, and as a result the South African government put churches under enormous pressure. Pityana's leadership during that crucial period was no doubt essential and strengthened the authority of the PCR internationally.

In 1982, the South African government ordered an investigation into the SACC by the Eloff commission, named after its chairman, Judge F. C. Eloff. Set up by the white government to control all aspects of the SACC's work, and initially to respond to alleged financial irregularities, it particularly inspected its sources of income from abroad. However, it soon became clear that the commission had received a much wider mandate and was being asked to examine the inception, development, objectives, and activities of the SACC, as well as its financial support. It interrogated not only members of the SACC staff but also of foreign aid agencies. In fact, early in 1983 an international delegation of church leaders went to South Africa to appear before the commission and testify about their experiences with the work of the SACC. In that same year, the WCC's assembly in Vancouver expressed its admiration and support for the prophetic and courageous stand taken by the SACC. In a statement on Southern Africa, the assembly said, "As a consequence of the life and witness of the Christians and the churches, there is unrelenting pressure on them and the SACC, most recently shown in the activities of the Eloff commission which appears to be an effort to muzzle and destroy the SACC."[15]

The WCC executive committee rejected the conclusions of the Eloff commission, drawing particular attention to its distorted understanding of church-state relations and to the SACC's ministry through humanitarian assistance and prophetic witness against oppression. And in 1984, the WCC central committee decided that

Southern Africa would remain a priority of the PCR. This was especially important in view of South Africa's attempts to create the misleading impression that it was now engaging in establishing peace in the region following the independence of Mozambique and Angola in 1975.

In that year, I was invited by the first Frelimo government to visit Mozambique as its guest. It was a time for me to remember Eduardo Mondlane, who, as the first president of Frelimo, had been so closely associated with the WCC during the 1960s before he was assassinated in 1969. After independence, his name was often used; for example, the University of Maputo was named after him. Nevertheless, one wondered whether his message of reconciliation was still alive among the new leaders of Mozambique.

9. At the ILO: 1982-1987

When I left the WCC, my wife and I decided we would, if possible, stay in Geneva (where we had lived since 1958), because our children and grandchildren were all living there. At the age of 55, finding a suitable job turned out to be not that easy. In the end, it was thanks to strong support from the Dutch mission to the UN in Geneva that I succeeded in getting a post at the International Labour Office (ILO). I started working there in January 1982 and was made responsible for the ILO's Anti-Apartheid Desk, which suited me well after my long experience at the WCC. I thought that maybe the ILO would be interested in exchanging ideas with the WCC and other NGOs about policies and programmes against apartheid.

However, I was not aware of the complicated situation in which the ILO found itself at that particular time. My predecessor in the Anti-Apartheid Programme, Neville Rubin, a lawyer from South Africa, had, according to a Report of the Commission of Inquiry into the Espionage Activities of the South African Government in the International University Exchange Fund (circulated in 1980), become entangled in secret bank relations involving funds for students in South Africa that were channelled through the International University Exchange Fund (IUEF), an organization whose main activity was providing students with scholarships. As I related in the last chapter, the IUEF was in turn infiltrated by Craig Williamson, a spy for the South African apartheid regime and an officer of the Special Branch of the South African Security Police. Williamson's information on South African applicants, passed on to the Pretoria regime, resulted in the arrest, imprisonment, and torture of many South African student-applicants. In addition, there is no doubt that his task was also, through the contacts of the IUEF, to try and infiltrate the ANC.

The IUEF had received several warnings about the real identity of Williamson, notably from the SACC. The ANC had also expressed concern. However, these warnings were not acted upon by IUEF's director, Lars-Gunnar Eriksson. Williamson's position in the IUEF made it possible for him to connect with a wide range of international and national organizations. He tried to contact the PCR but I was from the beginning reluctant and not convinced that he could be trusted. In 1979, we received a visit from an ANC official who asked us whether the PCR would be willing to help support the opening of an ANC office in Geneva by paying the rent – an office to be located on IUEF premises. I was astounded at the ANC's interest in having its office at the IUEF, but refrained from comment because I thought the ANC would be aware of existing doubts concerning Williamson's role in the IUEF.[1] Our response was that we never supported such direct projects by a liberation movement, but that the ANC, if it so wished, was of course free to use a grant by the PCR's Special Fund for such purposes.

However, the ILO became indirectly involved in the IUEF crisis because Rubin, according to the report, lent his support to one of the IUEF's secret projects related to Williamson. The Report of the Commission of Inquiry states that this project concerned a secret Liechtenstein company called Southern Futures Anstalt (Institution), which was created to hide deficits and overspending of the IUEF Geneva office as well as to use funds from donors, contributed for the relief of refugees and other projects, for administrative expenses of IUEF headquarters. Rubin, the report states, had cheque-signing powers in Southern Futures and had been involved in signing blank cheques as well as receiving fees for his services. This was contrary to ILO rules, according to which international civil servants "shall not engage in any political or other activity or occupation or hold any office which is incompatible with the proper discharge of their duties, and shall obtain the prior approval of the Director General before they engage in outside occupations."[2]

To the outside – and especially to NGOs like the WCC/PCR involved in anti-apartheid activities – the whole scandal stank. ANC officials told me afterwards that they felt betrayed by the IUEF.

When the scandal broke, Rubin was temporarily transferred to another ILO post in New York (later, in 1987, he became my successor). Thus, there was a vacancy in the Anti-Apartheid Desk which I filled for just over five years. I learned the details of my predecessor's problems only after my arrival and I then became aware that the IUEF scandal could put the ILO's future relations with the (Southern African) national liberation movements (NLMs) at risk. This was not the best way to start a new job in an organization I knew only from the outside.

An inauspicious beginning

The huge building of ILO, which employed a staff of between 2000 to 2500, was only a few hundred metres from the WCC (which employed only some 250 people), and I soon found out that the atmosphere was quite different from what I was accustomed to in the much smaller ecumenical organization. It was a huge bureaucracy.

The ILO is the oldest of the specialized UN organizations, created in 1919 as part of the Versailles Treaty that ended the first world war. As a tripartite organization of representatives of governments, independent employers, and workers unions, which is unique in the world of intergovernmental organizations, it reflected the belief that universal and lasting peace could only be achieved if it was based on social justice. Soon after its creation, the ILO was confronted with the Great Depression and its resulting massive unemployment. Amongst its most significant achievements are a number of fundamental human and trade-union rights conventions, like those on freedom of association (Convention 87, 1948) and the right to collective bargaining (Convention 98, 1949).

The ILO had taken some significant initiatives in the anti-apartheid field: for example, the annual International Labour Conference in 1964 had adopted a Declaration Concerning the Policy of Apartheid of the Republic of South Africa, which was accompanied by a Programme of Action. These two elements were the basis for the ILO's campaign, which would be sustained until the white Pretoria regime was finally removed in 1994. The declaration stipulated that there be an annual report on action against apartheid by the tripartite members, which would be presented and discussed by a special committee of the annual International Labour Conference.

My new superior, Claude Rossillion, a French lawyer in charge of the Equality of Rights Branch, told me on my very first day that in my new job I was preferably not to take fresh initiatives. Rather I should, he said, respond to the best of my ability to any questions that might be asked of me. This came like a cold shower. In the WCC a major responsibility was to produce new ideas and projects. Not so in the ILO; at least not in my job in the field of anti-apartheid. As I soon found out, "apartheid" was a hot potato. The organization's tripartite system had of course for many years expressed its strong opposition to apartheid (South Africa had been forced to leave the ILO in 1964 after the above-mentioned Declaration on Apartheid was adopted), especially because of South Africa's violation of fundamental workers and trade union rights, its cheap labour policies, and the scandalous conditions of black workers. But, as in the churches, the ways and means through which to help abolish apartheid were strongly disputed. Some governments, including those of the US and several Western European countries, and many employer organizations opposed strong action for a long time because they were in one way or another doing extensive business with South Africa. And even the trade unions were not of one mind: the International Confederation of Free Trade Unions and the communist inspired World Federation of Trade Unions did not see eye to eye. Some of their members supported newly created black and non-racial unions inside South Africa, like those affiliated to the Federation of South African Trade Unions (predecessor of the Congress of South African Trade Unions) and the Council of Unions of South Africa, which excluded white leadership, while others preferred to support unions or federations such as the South African Congress of Trade Unions (SACTU) with direct links to the ANC.

In the 1970s and the beginning of the 1980s an explosion of new initiatives in South Africa by the black workers themselves took place. The coming into being of these new unions, black as well as non-racial, should have alerted the ILO to consider new and constructive policies and programmes in support of these unions. It was well known that SACTU, created in 1955, was working only in exile and that they were no longer directly related to the recent trade-union developments inside the country. The situation inside the country was degenerating to such an extent that even some employers organizations urged stronger measures against the white regime. This should have incited the ILO to consider more direct support to these new unions, although it should be recognized that the technical cooperation programme launched in 1981 had at least one workers education project in support of the new unions inside South Africa and Namibia.

Surprisingly, my new colleague and closest collaborator in the office, Bill Ratteree, informed me that the staff union of the ILO was not happy with my appointment because it favoured promotion from inside the organization. Appointments from the outside ("parachutists"), and certainly from an NGO, were not encouraged. Again, this did not make for a happy start.

One day I found a cartoon in a newspaper depicting two men listening to each other intensely but unable to speak because they both had their mouths scotch-taped. That was how I felt; quite the opposite of the work atmosphere in the WCC. When Rossillion asked why I had pinned the cartoon on my door, I replied that I found it an interesting drawing. But he probably understood what I felt and advised me take it down, which I said I would not do as long as I was in that office. This set the tone of the relationship with my new boss. I had a difficult start in this job (later my relationship with my superior was normalized) because I had much less freedom than in the WCC. It was clear that practically nobody was interested in what I had done in the field of combating apartheid and racism before joining the ILO.

Just before leaving the WCC, I had produced a booklet entitled *Isolating Apartheid*,[3] giving a résumé of WCC action over the years through the PCR and what, in my opinion, should be done in the future. I thought, in my naivety, that this would give my new colleagues an idea of what I had been involved in and would be a basis for a fruitful exchange of views. But instead of expressing some kind of interest, their reaction was silence. A few months after my arrival, one of the employer's representatives on the ILO governing body, a compatriot of mine, Cornélie Hak, invited me for lunch. Her comments about my appointment left no doubt: had she known more about my background, she would have opposed it. At least her stance as an employer representative was clear from the beginning. So there I was – not really welcome!

Making my mark

But fortunately some staff colleagues encouraged me. It was largely through the support and close cooperation of Ratteree that things started to move, although only slowly. The strict hierarchical situation in an organization like the ILO was such that no quick decisions could be taken; every issue of some importance had to be referred higher up and would come back down the same hierarchical ladder with comments and questions, sometimes marked "strictly confidential" or "we spoke." Incoming external mail was always opened in the central mail office, even if it concerned letters marked "personal." Thus I would receive an invitation to speak at a German Evangelical academy which would already have been read and commented on by my superiors before it reached me! It was also known that the intelligence services of some big powers were interested in incoming and outgoing mail.

There was no doubt that I had to learn to work in a totally different environment and adapt myself to friendly diplomatic discourse if I wanted to get anywhere. Gone were the days of direct access to the general secretary and taking quick decisions myself. I only met ILO Director General Francis Blanchard once by chance in the elevator! When writing a project, I had to keep in mind the different sensitivities of the ILO's three major partners and adapt my language accordingly. Fortunately, Ratteree was there to help me find my way in this labyrinth: his wisdom and patience were fundamental to my survival.

But once I had accepted my new role and responsibilities, I decided I had to make my presence felt and put my imprint on at least a few things that I felt were essential for the ILO and for myself. My knowledge of and close relations with most of the NLMs could help the ILO to change its image. Its reputation with the movements badly needed to be improved after what had happened in relation to the Williamson scandal, which indirectly touched the ILO.

Because of the Cold War and the growing political crisis in Southern Africa in the 1980s there was a certain reluctance within the ILO to be seen to be too close to the NLMs. The lack of internal organization of some of the NLMs sometimes proved an obstacle to regular contact. We had been accustomed to this in the WCC. Most NLM offices and personnel were concentrated in the frontline states: Mozambique, Tanzania, Zimbabwe, Zambia, and Angola. So when the occasion arose to hold seminars with future trade-union leadership, it seemed logical to organize these seminars in those states. This suited the ILO, as it meant the meetings were less visible and less costly. But there was another reason: many of the participants were recruited from inside South Africa and Namibia without the knowledge of the Pretoria regime. They would never have been able to come to Europe without legal documents and visas; in the frontline states this could be worked out much more easily. The ILO could contribute to the necessary training of future union leadership and so we promoted the holding of regular trade-union seminars in cooperation with SACTU and the Pan Africanist Congress of Azania, as well as the South-West African People's Organization (SWAPO).

For these seminars to be held and in general to maintain regular contacts with the NLMs in the field and to support the implementation of ILO technical cooperation work, it was essential to have field staff. To this end, we recruited associate experts (that is, junior

ILO officials supported by certain donor governments in Europe) stationed in the frontline states. Originally several came from Norway. In 1983, we appointed Ms Judica Amri from Tanzania, to be stationed in Lusaka. In 1987 she was succeeded by Ms Elinor Sisulu from Zimbabwe/South Africa. Both of them worked closely with the NLMs locally and were responsible for preparing the seminars in consultation with the government of the host country. We also hired for each seminar the services of a competent consultant, specialized in the issues the trade unions had chosen to discuss. In order to give the meeting the necessary official status and clout, the minister of labour of the frontline state concerned would address the opening ceremony. I was under strict orders from headquarters to chair these meetings all along. But I felt that the workers needed to take their own responsibility for such meetings and choose their own chairperson. So I limited myself to presiding over the opening and closing ceremonies and for the rest of the time I was a participant and available if needed. This sign of confidence on our part was much appreciated by the leadership of the NLMs.

We reported annually on these seminars and also published a list of participants. It was clear, though, that the trade unionists from inside South Africa and Namibia who came without the knowledge of the South African government could not be named for fear of being arrested at home. So there was a tacit agreement with the NLMs that they would compose the list of participants themselves in order to avoid risks. But the United States mission in Geneva, probably acting on behalf of the South African mission, which no longer had direct access to the ILO, became suspicious. I received a visit from the US labour attaché in Geneva, who questioned me about the seminars. I replied that all this was written clearly in our annual reports. To which he replied that he knew that and he had also seen the lists of participants, but that he wanted their real names and their position in the NLMs. When I answered that all I could give him was the report, he said I was obstructing his inquiry and that he would report this to Francis Blanchard.

Another incident with the US mission took place during an annual labour conference when I was talking in the lounge to one of the representatives of SACTU, which was part of the ANC and a member of the (communist) World Federation of Trade Unions. Suddenly a photographer appeared and started taking pictures of us without having asked permission. When I protested and asked on whose behalf he was doing this, he said it was at the request of the US mission. I asked him to stop immediately and lodged a protest with the US mission which I sent to the director general (through all the necessary channels, of course!). It was clear to me that the Americans were collecting material that they could use against me.

One of the main activities of the Equality of Rights Branch, to which the Anti-Apartheid Desk belonged, was the annual report to the Special Committee on Action against Apartheid of the International Labour Conference on the labour situation in South Africa and measures taken by the ILO's constituencies to help abolish apartheid. This was a colossal job based on replies to a detailed questionnaire. All the answers had to be integrated into one document for presentation to the Special Committee for comment and discussion. Its preparation took months of solid work that neither Bill Ratteree nor I had the time for. Thus we hired the services of a special consultant who joined our staff temporarily for four or five months. We were fortunate to find Bill Vose, a former labour attaché of the British embassy in Pretoria, ready to undertake this special assignment for several years. The question each year was how to make these reports readable even when many of the answers were often a repetition of the previous years.

ILO priorities

Not long after I joined the ILO, I found that there was a plan in the director general's office to invite Gatsha Buthelezi, chief minister of the Kwazulu-Natal Bantustan, to address the 1986 annual labour conference as one of the keynote speakers. (In 1982, Buthelezi had received the George Meany human rights award from the American federation of trade unions AFL-CIO; the preceding year this award had gone to the Polish trade unionist Lech Walesa of Solidarnosc.)

Buthelezi had tried in 1986 to create his own trade union, the United Workers Union of South Africa, which was not to the liking of the other South African trade unions, but it never got off the ground. It was immediately clear to me that Buthelezi should not be invited as a speaker. Earlier, we had had experience with him in the WCC and we knew that he was a puppet of the Pretoria regime. I discussed the matter with my superiors, only to find out that Buthelezi was on good terms with the director general himself and that it would not be easy to change his mind unless I could convince him otherwise. This meant that I would have to make a convincing dossier. I also knew that such a dossier might be shared with some influential government representatives. It would therefore have to be an irrefutable argument. But it was not only a matter of not inviting Buthelezi; we had to see to it that in his place the highest authority of the ANC was invited as a speaker. An invitation to Oliver R. Tambo, the acting president of the ANC, to speak at the 1986 International Labour Conference would send a strong signal of the ILO's stance in regard to the anti-apartheid struggle. It was time for the ILO to accept the historic role which the ANC was playing in the liberation of the black majority of South Africa. With the help of friends from other organizations, I put together what was needed to "convert" the director general's office and I succeeded, but not without a lively exchange of memos and long discussions about the fact that Tambo should be invited instead of Buthelezi. Frankly speaking, I found it surprising that in the highest echelons of the organization they had not yet read the signs of the times.

Later, in 1988, Tambo was followed by Sam Nujoma, president of SWAPO of Namibia, and finally in 1990 by Nelson Mandela, very soon after his release from prison. After thanking the ILO for its support throughout the years, he had to remind the labour conference that the ILO needed to continue its pressure on the apartheid regime as long as it was in place.

Strangely enough, it looked as if apartheid was not on the list of ILO's top priorities. This seems confirmed in the memoirs of the director general[4] which do not mention the issue of apartheid at all, although almost all of the anti-apartheid programme work took place during his administration (1974-89), including the revision of the Declaration on Apartheid in 1989 (although Philippe Séguin in his foreword mentions apartheid in passing). Neither is there any mention of the speech by Tambo, nor of the severance of relations with the Union Bank of Switzerland (UBS), which was a very sensitive issue for the ILO.

Though not everyone was happy about the invitation to Tambo to speak at the 1986 labour conference, I felt this was a small personal victory. His invitation was also facilitated by the appointment in 1985 of Bulelani Ngcuka, from South Africa, as an intern in our branch. Ngcuka was a lawyer and an active member of the ANC. He had been imprisoned by the Pretoria regime for his activities and had to leave South Africa afterwards for safety reasons. His wife, Phumsile, already worked in Geneva with the World YWCA. It was important to have him in the office because we could consult directly with him on many matters: he was well informed. His insights and contacts with the ANC were most valuable.

But support for apartheid needed not only to be ended around the world; it was equally important to do away with it inside the ILO itself. Like the WCC, the ILO was dependent on the banking services of UBS, and the bank also had a branch in the building. With the help of the ILO staff union, which became a forum for efforts to get rid of the UBS, we started a campaign to end the services of the bank. This was a hard nut to crack, for the ILO was a big institution that depended heavily on UBS's specialized services. However, after prolonged negotiations, the administration agreed in 1985 to end its relations with the UBS and to use other banks for its substantial financial operations.

In 1984 I went to Angola for several weeks with one of my superiors, Pierre Adossama, a former cabinet minister from Togo. We were to inspect ILO technical cooperation projects with SWAPO. The internal situation in the country was unsafe and we had to rely on army protection throughout our trip. It was impressive to witness how upbeat the Namibians were in spite of the difficult situation at home, as well as in Angola. We met hundreds of SWAPO women and men in the different camps who were actively preparing for return home. And the ILO technical training facilities – for truck drivers, carpenters, blacksmiths, primary school teachers, and nurses – was one example, which we saw with our own eyes, of the high spirits of refugees living under difficult circumstances as they prepared (with the help of the ILO) to return home with a diploma. The ILO had provided building facilities and qualified teachers and instructors, who came mostly from Eastern Europe.

Five years later, in 1990, Namibia finally became independent. I was present during the splendid and moving ceremonies in the Windhoek stadium and by chance ran into some of the people I had met during my trip in Angola. Freedom from the illegal South African occupation had finally come for them.

As Adossama and I were staying in the same hotel in Luanda, we met at breakfast. To my surprise, he started talking about freemasonry and wanted me to read material he had brought with him. Now I had heard about freemasonry influence at the top echelons of the ILO, but I did not expect to be lectured about its importance on a field trip in Southern Africa! At one point Adossama asked whether I would be interested to know more about what was for him a particularly important issue and perhaps join his lodge, the "Grand Orient de France." I expected this and made clear to him that as a committed Christian I had no particular interest in joining one or other freemasonry lodges, particularly because it seemed such a secret affair. Later, I heard from a friend at the ILO that he too had been approached by freemasons and offered the opportunity to enter a lodge.

On 31 March 1987, my 60th birthday, I left the ILO. I was not at all ready for retirement – this new part of my life. Although the ILO offered a special course for future retired international civil servants, I didn't want to participate along with other people I didn't know well: I wanted to protect my privacy.

All in all, my five years at the ILO had not been easy. I never really got accustomed to the hierarchical structures of the organization. In addition, I was surprised and disappointed at the lack of commitment to social justice (which after all is the supreme goal of the ILO) of some of my colleagues in the higher echelons, who seemed more interested in promotion and still more in privileges as international civil servants, who are in any case already exempt from taxation.

It seemed to me that there also was a clear lack of cooperation on the issue of apartheid between the different UN organizations, as well as between the ILO and the NGOs, and notably the WCC. But on the other hand, and thanks to the support of a few colleagues at headquarters and in the field, we had been able to set things moving in the right direction, and I am grateful for that.

During my time at the ILO I never lost contact with my former colleagues at the WCC, and to my surprise Brigalia Bam, who was in charge of the WCC desk on men and women in church and society (later she became general secretary of the SACC, and subsequently she was made chairperson of the Independent Electoral Commission of South Africa), came to my farewell party and gave a brief but glowing speech, saying that it was perhaps not so bad for the ILO to have benefited from someone who came from an NGO like the WCC! Some chuckled at that as a sign of appreciation, but others looked nervous and critical. They were not accustomed to hearing such frank talk from the other side of the fence!

10. The Kairos Document: 1985

In 1985, as the crisis in South Africa continued to worsen, a turning point came from an ecumenical group of 151 lay and professional theologians in South Africa, representing a wide spectrum of denominations: Reformed, Lutheran, Anglican, Methodist, Baptist, Congregational, Evangelical, Pentecostal, and Roman Catholic. They published *The Kairos Document – A Challenge to the Churches: A Theological Comment on the Political Crisis in South Africa*.[1]

I was no longer working in the Programme to Combat Racism by then, of course, but the document proved of such capital importance that it has a place in my story. It was a watershed in the movement to resist apartheid and the struggle for liberation of Christians in South Africa. The impact of the document in fact went far beyond the country itself.

This group of Christians, both black and white, bluntly declared that

> the present regime has no moral legitimacy and is in fact a tyrannical regime ... the moral illegitimacy of the apartheid regime means that the church will have to be involved at times in civil

disobedience. A church that takes its responsibilities seriously in these circumstances will sometimes have to confront and to disobey the state in order to obey God ... the church of Jesus Christ is not called to be a bastion of caution and moderation. The church should challenge, inspire and motivate people.

The initiative for the document came from Frank Chikane, in charge of the Institute for Contextual Theology. At the outset, seven theologians and ministers got together in Soweto. Interestingly enough, one of them was white: Wolfram Kistner, who remembered how the discussion moved from the original idea to publish a statement in the institute's publication on the crisis, to making an analysis of the crisis and a theological commentary on the situation because of the incapacity of the churches to do so. It was urgent to frame a different biblical and theological model that could lead to a much-needed different kind of involvement by the churches. The original group widened gradually to involve people from all over the country, and no less than five drafts were circulated before the final text was approved and published. It is therefore clear that this text was the result not simply of a few people at the top but the product of broad involvement by groups at the grassroots.[2]

Kairos is "the moment of grace and opportunity, the favourable time in which God issues a challenge to decisive action." It is also a "reading [of] the signs of the times" (Matt. 16:3). The deeply biblical and prophetic words of the Kairos Document were based on the experience of millions of suffering people, particularly in the townships. The document was a contextual theological comment on the political situation in South Africa. It strongly criticized the churches' attitude toward apartheid and asked for a response and a definite choice, not only by individual Christians but also by the churches, which had so far neglected to speak out clearly or had even defended the system. It was a clear step toward a confessing church in a country completely divided by racism, and bore strong similarities to the Barmen Declaration by Christians of the Confessing Church in Germany (1934), when the Nazis took power and began persecuting the Jews and all those who were seen as the enemies of the *Herrenvolk* (the chosen people).

In South Africa, only a few individual Christians, like Archbishop Joost de Blank and the Rev. Beyers Naudé, had spoken out so far. The (coloured) Dutch Reformed Mission Church (DRMC) was the exception when it declared in 1982 in its Belhar Confession that the system of apartheid was an issue of *status confessionis*. But the DRMC's hands were tied: it was financially completely dependent on its so-called "mother church," the white DRC.

The Kairos Document has to be seen as an important step in the struggle against apartheid – a movement within all the denominations. The document had no official status. Its only authority was its strong spiritual and biblical content. It represented what millions of Christians, especially blacks, believed. It had an immediate impact on people who felt deserted by their churches and whose hope for a better future was at last clearly articulated. The black churches in South Africa were the churches of millions of the poor, but they had no authority in public life; they were discriminated against and powerless.[3]

The Kairos Document strongly criticized *state theology* as promoted by the apartheid state, which was seen simply as the theological justification of the status quo with its racism, law and order, capitalism, and fear of communism; it misused theological and biblical concepts (Rom. 13:1-7). The document also criticized *church theology*, which, though critical of apartheid, was naive and confused about reconciliation, justice, and peace. *Prophetic theology*, on the other hand, demanded a "bold and massive response that is prophetic because it speaks to the particular circumstances of this crisis." The document also criticized the lack of *political strategies* and *social analysis* and the use of absolute principles like reconciliation, negotiation, non-violence, and peaceful solutions, and their indiscriminate application to all situations.

The reasons for the crisis, the Kairos Document stated, must be sought in the type of faith and private, other-worldly spirituality that has dominated church life for centuries. "It is precisely this kind of spirituality that, when faced with the present crisis in South Africa, leaves so many Christians and church leaders in a state of paralysis." It had no biblical foundation.

The Bible does not separate the human person from the world in which he or she lives; it does not separate the individual from the social or one's private life from one's public life. God redeems the whole person as part of his whole creation (Rom. 8:18-24). A truly biblical spirituality would penetrate into every aspect of human existence and would exclude nothing from God's redemptive will. Biblical faith is prophetically relevant to everything that happens in the world.[4]

The chapter on social analysis made it clear that it would be wrong to define the conflict as simply a racial war. There was a racial component, but in the first instance it was a question of oppression: "the conflict is between an oppressor and the oppressed." The black majority was "no longer prepared to be crushed, oppressed and exploited. They are determined to change the system radically so that it no longer benefits the privileged few. And they are willing to do this even at the cost of their own lives. What they want is justice for all. This is our situation of civil war or revolution."[5]

Obedience to the state and *violence* were major issues in the Kairos Document. Regarding violence, an essential point was made that churches and the state both used and condemned violence indiscriminately. The state had chosen to call violence what young people did in the townships, that is, throwing stones or burning cars and buildings and sometimes killing collaborators. But this ignored all the structural and institutional violence of the state itself, committed especially by the army and the police.

Here, it should be added that the government also spoke of the violence of the ANC. But it forgot that this violence was in response to the violence of its system of apartheid. That system was forcing millions of people, because of the colour of their skin, to live in the townships or the so-called homelands without any infrastructure: they were treated like "cattle and dumped in homelands to starve – all for the benefit of a privileged minority." They were sent into the wilderness – a barbarous act of violence. In the South African situation, the issue was not whether there should or should not be violence; it was clear that the South African government only understood the language of violence. On the contrary, the issue had become one of trying to find a way out that might be the least violent and that respected the rights of people of every colour as much as possible. Since its creation in 1912, the ANC had tried to find a peaceful solution to the legitimate grievances of the black people. But the white minority regime had always refused to open the door for negotiation; instead, it hardened its policies of separate development each time.

One could argue that counter-violence should not happen in a mood of revenge: hatred never leads to a sense of community. But who were we as outsiders (often sitting on the fence) to dictate to the victims of apartheid what their legitimate demands and means to achieve them should be? The responsibility of the WCC member churches was in the first instance to try to remove the causes of violence. And in this respect we had so far failed miserably. The PCR had therefore been created to analyze these causes and to act, in order to help create conditions for community and for justice, and to make non-violence possible. Community cannot be created by separation. It asks for what African leaders like Julius Nyerere, Nelson Mandela, and Desmond Tutu have called *Ubuntu*, which means "I am because you are." Those who believe in apartheid had lost their own identity as human beings. Our Christian faith asks that our societies be inclusive in order to make it possible for all to live together.

The Kairos Document ended with a *message of hope* and a call for support:

> As the crisis deepens day by day, what both the oppressor and the oppressed can legitimately demand of the churches is a message of hope. Most of the oppressed people in South Africa today and especially the youth do have hope. They are acting courageously and fearlessly because they have a sure hope that liberation will come. Often enough their bodies are broken but nothing can now break their spirit. But hope needs to be confirmed. Hope needs to be maintained and strengthened. Hope needs to be spread. The people need to hear it said again and again that God is with them... We must participate in the cross of Christ if we are to have the hope of participating in his resurrection.[6]

Finally, the document called "upon our Christian brothers and sisters throughout the world to give us the necessary support in this regard so that the daily loss of so many young lives may be brought to a speedy end."[7]

The Kairos Document considerably strengthened the position of the WCC, and the PCR, delighted with this initiative, helped to disseminate the text worldwide.

11. The End of Apartheid Rule: The 1990s

The year 1990, toward the end of apartheid rule, brought the beginning of sweeping changes. Liberation movements were unbanned and political prisoners released. Nelson Mandela walked out of prison on 11 February 1990, after 27 years. In June of that year, he and his wife Winnie visited the WCC headquarters with a large ANC delegation. To a packed hall he paid a warm tribute to the work of the WCC over the years, in solidarity with the people of South Africa. For me personally, this was a moving and memorable moment. After the meeting, my wife Jet and I briefly met Mandela and Winnie in the general secretary's office. It was a strange moment because we were left alone without being introduced to the couple. There was the great man whom we only knew from out-of-date pictures and whose movement in- and outside South Africa, the ANC, we had supported for so many years. So I had to introduce the two of us, mumbling who we were and trying to start a discussion. Mandela understood my embarrassment and he repeated in a very personal way what he had said in the plenary meeting, while Winnie enthusiastically supported him.

What seemed impossible until recently was suddenly reality! As Desmond Tutu said, "We live with a God of surprises ... freedom is breaking out all over the place."[1] People who once demonized each other now sat at the same table to discuss the future of their country.

Successive events posed a challenge to some fundamental policy positions of the WCC. What did these events portend for South Africa? How would they affect the ministry of the churches in the country? What would the WCC's future role be? To try and answer these and other questions, PCR organized a consultative emergency meeting in Harare a few weeks after Mandela's release, to assess and interpret how these developments would affect WCC policy against apartheid. The meeting listened to the voices of the churches in South Africa and to the views of the liberation movements. The need to maintain international pressure against the system was felt to be essential in order to force the government to start meaningful negotiations as soon as possible. Frank Chikane, general secretary of the SACC, underlined the continued role for the international church community. The WCC had mainly worked through SACC, but it realized the importance of widening its contacts through the Southern African Catholic Bishops Conference (SACBC), the trade unions COSATU and NACTU, and a number of grassroots organizations.

Significantly, the churches of South Africa came together at Rustenburg in November 1990, under the title "Towards a United Christian Witness in a Changing South Africa." The meeting was also attended by church leaders from other parts of the world. Prominent Dutch Reformed (DRC) theologians publicly confessed their complicity in the sin of apartheid. Indeed, all the white church leaders admitted that, at the very least, they had sinned by omission through excessive impartiality. Given the South African context, the meeting was a historic as well as a political event. At Rustenburg, Beyers Naudé, who had suffered so much over the years from the attitude of his own church (DRC), apologized to the WCC for the injustice done to it:

> My deep conviction [is] that an apology from the DRC is due to the WCC for the serious wrong which it did to this world ecumenical body in 1961. But an official apology is also due to the

ecumenical movement throughout the world where the National Party propaganda deliberately made the WCC the scapegoat of its own anger at the resolutions adopted at Cottesloe. For decades, the nationalist propaganda machine deliberately created and sustained a totally distorted image of the WCC and of its important ecumenical role. For the sake, not of the World Council, but of the DRC and its acceptance in the ecumenical fellowship, there is dire need for this church to state its sincere regret to the World Council for this unfortunate development. How easy it would be to say: "We are sorry. Forgive us."[2]

Apartheid was not dead. Reconciliation was called for between churches and conflicting groups in the nation. The Rustenburg meeting called for an effective monitoring system on violence to be supervised by an international group with adequate powers to investigate report and ensure appropriate action.

The 7th Assembly of the WCC in 1991 in Canberra was less preoccupied with Southern Africa than previous assemblies. But PCR did organize a small brainstorming meeting on the situation in South Africa during the assembly, which posed some critical questions about the churches' responsibility in the interim period preceding a post-apartheid society. Apartheid and the struggle against it had fostered a "culture of violence," stated a paper prepared for the meeting, quoting the observation by Frank Chikane that the most tragic reflection of the war situation in which South Africa found itself was that it faced the years to come with children who had been socialized to find violence completely acceptable and human life cheap. The current situation could not be understood without acknowledging that it was the result of the long and brutal tyranny of dehumanization by apartheid. And the paper added that the church must now actively engage in addressing and eliminating poverty, providing adequate health, welfare, and educational facilities. Hitherto, part of the church had focused mainly in the political battle to dismantle apartheid. As rapid changes were taking place, the church needed to involve itself now in the socio-economic situation, highlighting the problems by making a theological analysis.

The assembly itself recognized in a statement on South Africa,

> The liberation struggle, as well as boycotts, economic sanctions
> and other measures which have served to isolate South Africa from
> the world community of nations, have combined to   produce a
> growing momentum for change. It is already becoming evident,
> however, that the next phase in the movement for a new, demo-
> cratic and non-racial South Africa might yet prove to be the most
> difficult phase of all.[3]

While many apartheid laws were being abolished, the discrimina-
tory structures and practices that had created them remained intact.
In particular, the government had made no commitment to a policy
of fair and just redistribution of land.

An important moment came in October 1991, when WCC General Secretary Emilio Castro visited South Africa at the invitation of
the SACC: it was the first visit to the country by a WCC general secretary since 1970. There were many occasions of ecumenical mourning as well as rejoicing. Castro met President F. W. de Klerk as well
as Nelson Mandela and other leaders of the ANC, the Pan Africanist Congress of Azania, the Azania People's Organization, and the
Inkatha Freedom Party, appealing to the leaders to do everything in
their power to help end the violence in the country.

The visit ended in Cape Town with a jointly sponsored SACC-
WCC consultation, "Towards an Ecumenical Agenda for a Changing
South Africa," attended by church leaders from around the world.
The "honeymoon" period after the release of Nelson Mandela and
the unbanning of the liberation movements in 1990 was over. The
meeting called for "an effective monitoring system" on violence to
be supervised by an international group with adequate powers to
investigate, report, and ensure appropriate action. This appeal was
strengthened in May 1992 at a SACC-sponsored emergency summit
on violence, in which leading politicians and church people participated. It was clear that the churches could perform a role that no other
group could undertake – a role that could be made more credible by
international participation. This was important because the SACC's

own integrity had to be beyond question. It could not afford to be perceived as taking sides with any political group. In South Africa a great deal was expected of the WCC. Political movements and trade unions had emphasized the continuing role of the WCC at this critical stage, especially its possible contribution to monitoring the violence. Above all, the WCC could support the churches in South Africa in their efforts to prepare for a new stage in the country's history.

In answering the call of the Rustenburg meeting for an international monitoring system, an Ecumenical Monitoring Programme in South Africa (EMPSA) started its work in 1992. It was a joint venture of the SACC, the SACBC, and the WCC, but worked in close cooperation with similar UN, European Union, Commonwealth, and OAU efforts. It was their joined responsibility to monitor violence, negotiations, and the electoral process leading up to the first democratic elections in 1994. Initially, only ecumenical teams from churches in Canada, Denmark, Finland, Germany, Kenya, the UK, and the US were involved. Later, monitors from many other countries joined in. It was a tremendous effort, and the organizing of well-trained people was not always easy. It happened under great pressure. The programme started before there was a functioning administration, which led to considerable overwork. Difficulties also arose when both the Geneva and Johannesburg offices of EMPSA had to coordinate the screening, training, accommodation, and deployment of some 300 peace monitors. In spite of this, the general feeling was that EMPSA, which was operational from 1992 until after the first democratic elections in 1994, made a sizeable contribution to the overall South African process for peace. A report of the Ecumenical Eminent Persons Group to the WCC and the SACC states,

> It is because EMPSA has been with the people during the turbulent period of violence and the difficult stage of negotiations that it gained the confidence and respect of the communities. It is this confidence that made it possible for them to be of assistance at all stages of the electoral process. They took creative initiatives and intervened where necessary with sensitivity and care to enable and facilitate polling in many stations. They carefully monitored all

aspects of the elections... EMPSA has become a highly successful and significant ecumenical experience from which lessons and models can be drawn for other situations...It is ecumenism at work.[4]

In September 1993, Nelson Mandela, addressing the UN Special Committee against Apartheid, officially called for the end of most sanctions against his country. The implications of this decision for the anti-apartheid movement worldwide, and not least for the churches and the WCC, were considerable. The WCC's long-standing policy of supporting sanctions was reviewed by its central committee meeting in Johannesburg in January 1994.

Recognizing the need for translating the vision of a new South Africa into innovative and workable models, the SACC and the SACBC, the Institute for Contextual Theology, and Kagiso Trust, anticipating the end of sanctions, convened a conference in February 1992 entitled "Towards a Code of Investment Ethics for South Africa's International Economic Relations." Following the meeting, the SACC and SACBC created a task force on economic matters, composed of prominent South African theologians and economists. These and other initiatives by the churches in South Africa had the full support of the ecumenical movement.

However, the question soon became for the WCC, as a world ecumenical body, whether this dramatic highly concentrated attention on one area of the world, and specifically one country, could be maintained much longer in view of its many other responsibilities.

12. Elections in South Africa: 1994

As the first democratic elections in South Africa approached, the EMPSA teams were enlarged and I was asked by the WCC to join as one of the international monitors. It became a great historical occasion. As I wanted our local Swiss church congregation to be aware of what was happening, at a Sunday church service I asked them to send me "on mission." On my return I gave an account of my experience during a Sunday worship service. Similarly, the synod of the Reformed Church in Geneva invited me to talk about my experiences at one of its sessions.

And there was indeed a story to tell! South Africa was liberating itself from centuries of oppression. The unthinkable was happening. No one had expected that we would witness this moment in our lifetime. While preparing for the elections, the country was trying to come to grips with increasing violence. Thousands of South Africans had died over the previous years and numbers had been increasing daily. Negotiations for the transfer of power from the white government to the ANC had offered an opportunity to avoid descent into complete anarchy, but the violence still threatened to derail the prospects of a negotiated peace. Over the years, state violence committed by the white government was responsible for the deportation of millions of black people to the so-called homelands, large arid spaces with no infrastructure – a kind of desert. The regime had also been responsible for the assassination of many of its opponents and aimed at destabilizing the liberation movement in every possible way. Innocent people had been targeted in an attempt to ruin their lives and stir up tension between communities and political groups in order to sow conflict. In despair, the liberation movement had used counter-violence. These different kinds of violence had been extensively documented.

As the elections approached, there were several prime obstacles. One was Chief Gatscha Buthelezi of Kwazulu Natal and his Inkatha Freedom Party. Another was the extreme (white) right, which was involved in last-minute attempts to destabilize the ANC. This created insecurity in different parts of the country and thousands of innocent black people were killed. The ANC entered into negotiations with General Constant Viljoen, former head of the South African Defence Force, who demanded the establishment of a *volkstaat,* in which Afrikaans churches, culture, and language would be preserved. Cynically, someone suggested Robben Island as the only possibility! But there was no area in which Afrikaners were in a majority. In the end, Viljoen agreed to participate in the elections, leading his Freedom Front. In the case of Buthelezi, however, the ANC took the hard line, attempting to diminish the power of regional leaders vis-à-vis the centre. He held out till the last possible moment, but in the end, under strong international pressure – notably from the Kenyan ambassador, Henry Kissinger and Lord Carrington – he too agreed to participate in the elections. The ballot papers had already been printed, and millions of stickers had to be produced and attached in a great hurry in order to include the Inkatha party.

The SACC certainly had good reason to address a special letter to all South African Christians calling for prayer services to be held throughout the country. It spoke of an "epoch-marking event for which many have given their lives ... the sense of destiny fills us with awe. We must listen to Immanuel, God-with-us."

Witnessing South Africa's first democratic elections

When I arrived in Johannesburg on 16 April 1994, I had the strange feeling that I was entering the "Promised Land": South Africa, a place we had been forbidden entry to all these years; a place that all those struggling for so long in solidarity with the oppressed people had dreamed about. They dreamed that one day it would be a place of peace; that the walls of separation would be torn down; that people of all shades would finally be one, would laugh, cry, and live and work together for a better future. I had never thought in my wildest dreams that I would live to see that day! Not in our generation. While overflying Africa during the night I had wondered whether this dream might not be in danger of becoming a nightmare. Would the negotiated compromise between Mandela and his team and the white regime of de Klerk hold? Was there a booby-trap somewhere that would still set the whole edifice on fire, as many had feared earlier? Were we going to "monitor" heaven or hell?

This was the land originally of the Khoikhoi and the San, which my Dutch forefathers had conquered centuries ago. It had become a bulwark of a white orthodox Calvinist minority at the expense of millions of black people.

A week for orientation

On arrival at Jan Smuts airport, I was met by Horst Kleinschmidt, whom I knew from his time in London as the director of the International Defence and Aid Fund for South Africa (I had served as one of its board members). In his opinion, the elections would take place in a reasonably peaceful climate, with the possible exception of Natal and a few incidents in the other provinces. Natal was causing much headache: Buthelezi and his cronies of the Inkatha party were still refusing to take part in the elections and organizing violent incidents, killing and wounding many people in different parts of the country. The Right and the military were too divided to be a real danger. Diplomats seemed to agree with Kleinschmidt's prognosis.

There was tremendous excitement mixed with realism everywhere.

The next day we learned that Buthelezi's Inkatha Party would hold a big demonstration in front of Shell House (the headquarters of the ANC) in Johannesburg, in commemoration of those who died in an earlier incident with the ANC. If indeed it was held, it would no doubt provoke the ANC to counter-violence. The white government refused permission for the meeting, calling on Buthelezi to discipline his followers, while the ANC said it would defend its offices if they were attacked. In the end, Buthelezi decided to postpone the meeting, but there was strong police presence everywhere. Later, we learned that Buthelezi had finally agreed to participate in the elections, and people in the streets expressed their joy and hoped that violence would finally die down – Inkatha had killed thousands of people during the preceding months.

I went to Shell House and, despite heavy security, succeeded in entering. It was quite an experience to be in the building of what had been a liberation movement, had become a political party, and was on the way to becoming a government. I met Gene Ginwala, one of the top ANC officials, whom I knew from her time of exile in London. Somewhat to my surprise, she told me she hoped that the ANC would only get a relatively small majority and that there would be a strong opposition in parliament in order to make democracy work. A small majority would also spur the ANC to a much-needed clean-up of its own ranks. Afterwards, I took part in an interfaith meeting for peace, with Buddhists, Hindus, Muslims, Jews, and Christians praying together. There was indeed much reason for praying: even the smallest incident could destroy the momentum. Fortunately, however, the faith of the black people that "now was the time" was too strong to be side-tracked.

The next day we went to the central offices of the Independent Election Commission (IEC) in Johannesburg and met Frank Chikane, who was one of the sixteen IEC commissioners. It was impressive to see how more than one thousand people were working day and night to prepare for the first democratic elections! Later I met my former colleague and friend Brigalia Bam, now interim general secretary of the SACC. I helped her to make a list of special guests from abroad to be invited for the inauguration of the new state president, once elected.

Brigalia shared her concern about the future of the SACC. What shape should it take after years as a central leader resisting apartheid? Some were saying that the themes of resistance and reconciliation would have to be replaced by reconstruction and development; the SACC would have to be decentralized in order to be closer to the people and their needs. Reconciliation and the healing of wounds would in any case have to remain one of the main future challenges for the nation as a whole. Several people emphasized the problems for black Christians after the elections, when they would no longer be united in their resistance to the white regime but divided among their own different political parties. Then there was also the burning issue of land ownership for black farmers.

And what kind of an ecumenical agenda should there be after the elections? Parochialism was visible everywhere in many churches. Beyers Naudé, Wolfram Kistner, and Theo Kotze, through their Christian Institute, had with unbelievable courage and perseverance witnessed the ever more critical situation under apartheid in their country. The institute had played a key role in explaining developments in South Africa to the outside world, and these men of God called unceasingly on Christians around the world not to let down the oppressed blacks of South Africa and to put every possible pressure on the Pretoria regime. At home they had been considered all these years as heretics and traitors to the white cause.

When I met them, they made me aware of their doubts about the continuation of the Christian Institute. Would it still have a role after the elections? As always, Beyers was upbeat. He told me of the merger on April 14-15 of two Reformed Churches (the Dutch Reformed Mission Church and the Dutch Reformed Church in Africa) into a Uniting Reformed Church in Southern Africa at a special meeting in Cape Town. To everybody's surprise, the ceremony was attended by an uninvited guest: Nelson Mandela. He wanted to show how important this event was for the wider life of South Africa. He sat at the back of the hall but was immediately recognized, of course. Delegates first showed some reservation about his presence, but eventually he was cordially received. At the end, and as a sign of reconciliation, Mandela took part in the eucharist. The two churches that were uniting were established in 1857 as racial churches for black people and people of mixed race by the white Dutch Reformed Church. Their uniting was a sign of reconciliation for the nation, and Mandela wanted to acknowledge this through his presence. Beyers was adamant that from now on the key issue for the churches and the whole nation had to be "reconciliation."

The next day I flew to Cape Town and met Barney Pityana, Michael Lapsley, and Charles Villa-Vicencio. We discussed the political situation as it was developing in these days before the elections, and had a heated debate about Archbishop Desmond Tutu's decision that no Anglican clergy should be members of a political party. Eighty Christians – among them Barney Pityana and several other Anglican priests – published a full-page advertisement in the newspapers calling on Christians to vote for the ANC. Later we met former Jamaican Prime Minister Michael Manley, who was to head the Commonwealth election monitors; he had been one of the keynote speakers at the WCC's 1975 assembly in Nairobi. Together we went to Cape Town University to attend an ANC rally packed with over a thousand students to hear a flamboyant speech by Allan Boesak. Cries of *amandla* (power) and "down with the racist the National Party" sounded loudly.

Then we visited several townships (Kayelitsha, Langa, and Guguletu) to meet some of the church leaders we knew there, and were reminded of the extreme poverty of many black people. The courage of these men and women was unbelievable. At Theo and Helen Kotze's home we were joined by Margaret Nash, an old-timer of the Student Christian Movement, and we again discussed the future of the Christian Institute.

Back in Johannesburg, Beyers Naudé, as chairman of EMPSA, and I went to the airport to welcome the WCC monitors. Kenneth Kaunda, former president of Zambia, had accepted to lead the

Ecumenical Eminent Persons' Group as part of EMPSA, which was formed of 290 members. We had our first briefing session at the SACC. Several of us (Ninan Koshy/India, Ian Linden/UK, Wim van der Zee/Netherlands, Nora Chase/Namibia, Barthold Witte/Germany, Daniel Ntoni-Nzinga/Angola, and myself) were assigned to the most densely populated area, Pretoria-Witwatersrand-Vaal (PWV), operating from Johannesburg. We received our blue identification jacket and cap with the initials EMPSA, which we were to wear any time we were on duty.

It took some time for the members of our group (whose rapporteur I was) to get to know each other, since we were all rather outspoken! We were at all times responsible to the national coordinator and were to receive our instructions from him. Prior to our arrival we had signed a letter of understanding with the WCC that outlined our conditions of work and our responsibilities. We had daily local and regional debriefings and were thus informed of the latest developments; each group was provided with transportation and radio communication; any incidents or violence had to be reported immediately to the national coordinator; we were not allowed to move alone while on duty. It was hoped that our mere presence would have a calming effect. Most importantly, we were always guided by respected local people who knew the local situation exactly. We were informed about which other monitoring teams were operating in the same area and we were to make sure to cooperate with them.

We not only needed to know the elections rules, but also the geographical parameters, the exact location of the different polling stations, the role of the police and the army, what to do in case of emergency, and what was expected from us in terms of reporting. We visited polling stations in squatter camps and discovered that several were not yet equipped; for example, telephone lines were still being installed. Exchanging experience with other monitors was essential.

We went to a voter registration centre near the town of Vereeniging and watched hundreds of people already queuing up to have their photograph and fingerprints taken. Processing was very slow, and at first everyone was in high spirits and there was a lot of singing. But after a while the crowd became nervous and we had to ask local pastors and priests to intervene and explain, with the aid of loudspeakers, why they had to wait so long. This did not really help. The crowds became even more agitated and finally broke through the fences and streamed onto the compound. We discussed the difficulties with other monitors and local authorities and met Frank Chikane to report on what we had seen. He was under tremendous pressure and told us that there were similar situations elsewhere. Reports came in of bomb blasts and armed attacks on several polling stations in our area, probably the work of extreme white groups. Later it was reported that some 20 people had been killed and 150 injured in and around our area.

But nobody seemed to be frightened off – the elections would take place whatever the cost! The last political rallies were still being held, and most people seemed to know who to vote for. Many had still not been issued with identity papers for the elections, simply because there were no records. Fortunately, people could vote in the polling station of their choice. Some were afraid that the vote would not be secret: intimidation and violence were still prevalent. On the Sunday preceding the elections, special services were held all over the country. Our EMPSA monitors group went to a service in a township some 45 minutes east of Johannesburg; the church was packed and the service lasted more than three hours.

The election days

On April 26, the elections began. This was the voting day for the police and prisoners, as well as for the old and the sick in hospitals and homes. For the first time we wore our special jackets marked "international church monitors for peace." In Alexandra Township, some 15 kilometres from Johannesburg and famous for its long resistance against forced removals, we were met by the Rev. Sam Buti, well known by everyone there. We were witnesses of a very moving event when hundreds of sick, crippled and old people, partly bedridden, waited to vote for the first time in their lives. Amidst the people there we said prayers of thanksgiving that this day had finally come, and we thought about all those who had struggled for so long but who had not been allowed to see this day.

When we came outside, people were joyful but tense. Everywhere it was the same story: people waiting for hours in the cold while nothing seemed to move. Later, inside the polling station, we watched blind and disabled people express their party preference in the presence of party agents and the presiding officer, who then put a cross for them on the ballot paper. They arrived at the ballot box on wheelchairs, make-shift stretchers, crutches, some clutching saline drips. It took endless time, but it was so important to see how these people were allowed to vote in dignity. What an extraordinary and moving moment! Outside we talked to people in the queue and explained what was happening inside and why it took so long. They seemed to accept, knowing their turn would come eventually. People wanted to shake hands and greeted us with expressions of hope and jubilation. One man was reported demanding to know where he should put his mark for Jesus; he should surely be forgiven for believing that our Saviour was among the twenty or so fuzzy pictures of political party leaders decorating the huge ballot paper!

Never in my life had I watched people voting with such fervour and such conviction! Even the criminals seemed to be hypnotized by the wave of goodwill that swamped the country. Crime, according to police reports, fell by some 50 percent. A one-day public holiday became two; a three-day election became four. When ballot papers for some 22 million registered voters ran out, more ballot papers were printed. We visited the civic resource centre, another polling station in Alexandra Township, where the situation was chaotic. Several of us were squeezed like sardines in the crowd as we tried to get inside the building.

Afterwards we met in the local YMCA of Soweto. The chairperson of Ministers United for Christian Reconciliation described to us the years of resistance by the churches in different periods. The decade of the 1970s-80s had been critical. The Black Conscience Movement at one point took over leadership in the township when all other leaders were arrested, underground, or in exile. The 1976 children's revolt in Soweto – known as the Soweto Uprising – was an expression of the impotence of the elder generation. Children took it upon themselves to act: protest and solidarity politics, not education but liberation! And the chairperson added, "While the apartheid defenders quoted Romans 13, we quoted the Book of Revelations." He continued,

That was our state of mind. Now we will have to redefine our role as churches. Evil will stay. The church will have to remain on the alert – it could become co-opted by the new political system. Soon there will be divisions between us blacks. Many of us will remain illiterate and will have no access to the health system. Empowerment is a long way off. But we should not fall into the danger of reactionism. For now, we are fully mobilized for the elections! We need to discover a moral grounding for the new nation. The corruption of the old white system should not be allowed to creep into the new. We need to bring back the culture of learning and respect.

From Alexandra, we went to Diepkloof, Johannesburg's main prison with some 7000 inmates. We were divided into two groups, one for the male and one for the female section. I went to the female section and was able to speak to many women in the courtyard waiting their turn to vote. They were excited and wanted to know how people were voting in town. We were able to explain to some thirty women why they were not entitled to vote (they had committed murder, robbery, and violence); parliament during its last session, under pressure from de Klerk, had decided only the previous day which prisoners could or could not vote and the prison authorities had failed to inform them. It was difficult for us to convince them and it was not really our task.

Meeting these women brought us in touch with some human tragedies. One was a single mother of five children, who were left at home alone. She had been unable to pay her electricity bills, she said, and had received a ten-year sentence for robbery; she was only in her third month. She feared for her children (between 9 and 18 years old). Fortunately, one of our members, a bishop from Lesotho, took it upon himself to contact the parish of this woman. Other women were upset by the decision not to allow them to vote, and wanted to know whether a new government would give them amnesty. In the male section, things were worse. Police officers behaved brutally and prevented eligible prisoners from voting; we reported this to the responsible election commissioner in the area, Mrs Helen Suzman. In the evening we were able to share our observations also with Beyers Naudé and Sheena Duncan.

The next day we went 150 kilometres east of Johannesburg to Standerton (85,000 inhabitants, of which 15,000 whites), a small Afrikaner (Boere) town known to be ultra-conservative. One of the candidates of General Viljoen's Freedom Front Party, which claimed a *volksstaat* (a homeland) for the whites, came to explain their philosophy – very nostalgic. Despite threats if they did not get what they wanted, they were prepared to negotiate, and said they would not resort to violence if their demands were not met. Then we also saw the town mayor, a Dutch Reformed minister who received us in the town hall and with whom we very quickly clashed in theological debate. His argument was that a state composed of different nations was to be compared with the Tower of Babel. This was evil in God's eyes and He had confused and dispersed them because they didn't obey him. His examples in contemporary history were the USSR and Yugoslavia. In his view, each tribe should have its own homeland. Nora Chase, Namibian ambassador in Bonn, had to make an end to this debate, during which both Wim van der Zee (secretary of the Dutch Council of Churches) and I had great difficulty keeping our tempers – it was quite a session! Then we went to the different polling stations. Again, it was impressive to see thousands of black people walking from the townships to vote in the white town centre, to the amazement of the white farmers and their families. White and black were queuing together for hours and they were quite disciplined. In the town hall we discovered, however, that the used (full) ballot boxes were waiting unsealed and uncontrolled for transportation to central counting stations. The officers in charge told us they had run out of seals. New ones had been ordered but had not arrived, so some of the monitors agreed to guard the boxes as long as necessary.

Meanwhile reports came of an explosion at Johannesburg airport that had caused considerable damage. Later we were informed that

31 white extremists had been arrested in relation to the bomb blasts of the recent days. Another report spoke of the complaints of Gatcha Buthelezi about the slow voting in Natal-Kwazulu, his "homeland." He also complained about serious mistakes in vote recording. This, we felt, was his own fault since he had decided only five days earlier that he would participate in the elections. But it was important to avoid him withdrawing.

We inspected several other polling stations and were confronted with the question of what would happen after the election results were announced. Black people had been united in their resistance against apartheid for so long. Now that they were freely expressing their preferences, would they respect the results and accept the opinion of others? Democracy was a totally new concept for them (and indeed for the whites!).

The voting stations had to be guarded overnight and the ballot boxes had to be brought to safe places. Monitors were not keen to work during the night, given a lack of security. It was becoming clear that many people would not be able to vote because they would not receive their papers in time. Counting the votes had now begun. This was the moment monitors had to be especially alert. Our group of seven was assigned to observe closely at specific polling stations. We could, of course, witness only a tiny part of what was happening in this big country.

Counting the votes: First reactions and celebrating the results

By April 30, the voting was over, but the counting of the votes by the Independent Electoral Commission continued. In view of the many complaints about irregularities in the process and the count, there was a long way to go before the election could be declared "substantially free and fair." On May 3, only 51 percent of the votes had been counted, three days after the polling stations closed. There were many technical problems, which were criticized all round.

However, the results showed a clear trend. Of the total eligible population, 86 percent had voted. The ANC would have 62-65 percent of the votes, revealing a substantial victory, versus the white National Party with some 24 percent. But as was clearly emphasized at a meeting of religious leaders, which we as monitors attended, "the winners of the elections are the people who waited stoically for endless hours – both white and black in the same queue." This picture had never been seen in South Africa's history! And what was more, there had been no violence of any significance. The unanimous opinion was that we had witnessed a miracle.

That the ANC would not get a two-thirds majority in parliament was no doubt a blessing for democracy in the country. Had they obtained more than 66.6 percent they would have been able to change the interim constitution. The setback for the ANC came in the Western Cape Provence, where the ANC regional chairman Allan Boesak conceded defeat to the National Party. The Western Cape was the only province out of the nine in which black South Africans were in a minority.

Both de Klerk and Mandela made official statements after the results became clear. De Klerk acknowledged defeat and announced his resignation. He congratulated Mandela, stating that he was ready to work with him in a government of national unity. He called Mandela

> a man of destiny [who] has walked a long road and now stands at the top of the hill. A traveller would sit down and admire the view. But a man of destiny knows that beyond this hill lies another and another. The journey is never complete. As he contemplates the next hill I hold out my hand in friendship and in cooperation.[1]

De Klerk had showed himself magnanimous. Already in 1990 he had demolished the old Afrikaner vision of a white South Africa, of a *volksstaat* that was theirs by divine right and without which they could not survive as a national entity. He had ensured that in its stead a new black-led South Africa would arise, as alien to traditional Afrikaner thinking as Palestinian rule is to the Israelis. For the previous fifty years, especially, this "white tribe of Africa," as the three million or so Afrikaners are sometimes called, had seemed in the grip of an ethnic paranoia. They had been living at the southern tip of Africa for three and a half centuries and had come to regard themselves as indigenous. During their long sojourn in this remote place, their filial ties with Holland, from which most originally came, had withered to almost nothing: their Dutch had mutated into a new language, which they called Afrikaans, and their version of the Dutch Reformed Church had changed on the arid African *veld* into something more earthy and fundamentalist – a fire-and-brimstone faith that addressed the harsh circumstances in which they struggled to survive with the gun in one hand and the Bible in the other. South Africa was their God-given homeland, the place that gave them their national identity, and if ever they were forced to share it with the black majority it would cease to be theirs and that would be the end of them, for they could conceive of no nation surviving without a homeland. They therefore equated racial integration with "national suicide." De Klerk was motivated by very different concerns. He "did not expect his reforms to lead to black-majority rule and the end to Afrikaner nationalism before the end of the decade ... There could be no 'winner takes all' system, majority rule."[2]

In his statement as the first election results came in, de Klerk made it immediately clear that the ANC would be unable to rule without him and the National Party. In fact, he was warning Mandela: you will depend on me, I have the army, police, and the civil servants behind me. He also made it clear that he would contest the next elections in 1999, which he expected to win. In his electoral campaign, de Klerk claimed that he had ended apartheid and that the "new" National Party could not be blamed for the sins of the past. Although it is true that de Klerk, who would become the second vice-president, has earned a special place for himself in South Africa's history, his readiness to negotiate came at a time when the apartheid regime had run out of support from the outside, notably from the West. To this must be added the end of the international context of the Cold War, the fall of the Berlin wall, and the defeat of communism. As a result, NATO no longer needed to protect the Cape Route, which had been strategic for the defence of its interests. One should also not forget that apartheid South Africa had lost the war it initiated in Angola, which received military support from Cuba. All these elements meant that de Klerk's position was seriously undermined. The claim that the ruling white class gave power voluntarily to the black majority distorts history and denies the success of the liberation struggle, which received so much solidarity from the worldwide anti-apartheid movement, including the churches and the WCC.

Mandela, on his part, was no less a magnanimous statesman when he made his acceptance speech to a jubilant crowd. He expressed the emotions of millions of South Africans:

> I stand here before you, filled with deep pride and joy – pride in the ordinary, humble people of this country. You have shown such a calm, patient determination to reclaim this country as your own. And joy that we can loudly proclaim from the rooftop: "free at last" … This is the time to heal the old wounds and build a new South Africa.[3]

This was said by a man who had been sent to prison for 27 years by the apartheid regime, which he had now defeated not by the barrel of the gun but by the ballot box. Never did he say a word of bitterness about his past treatment. Mandela also held out a hand to the leaders of the other parties who lost the elections, including the Pan Africanist Party (PAC) and the Freedom Front, asking them to join him in working together to tackle the problems facing the nation. "An ANC government will serve all the people of South Africa, not just ANC members."[4] It was already becoming clear that Mandela's international stature would give him the chance to become the interlocutor between the developed and under-developed worlds, as they were then called.

Astonishingly enough, it was the two political leaders who showed the lead in a new process of reconciliation and healing of the nation. The churches had not yet followed suit. What were they waiting for? The big uncertainty and fear was that Gatscha Buthelezi and his Inkatha Freedom Party would not accept the election results if the ANC won in their fief Natal-Kwazulu. Some angry young men from Inkatha were already predicting that losing the elections would mean war. At the regional level there was a power vacuum. The old "homelands" no longer existed after April 27, but the new provincial structures were not yet in place. The new constitution stated that in the interim period all existing administrations would continue to function until repealed or amended. One ANC lawyer commented on this by saying that there would be "lots of cock-ups, plenty of confusion, a fair amount of corruption and a great deal of frustration. But in the end we'll muddle through – we always do."[5]

The ANC invited all the monitors and observers to celebrate their victory on the evening of May 2 at the Carlton Hotel in Johannesburg. "We are free, free at last and we thank God for it," said Thabo Mbeki, chairman of the ANC and the new first deputy president. And Nelson Mandela spoke of the excluded people – black, Asians, and coloured (mixed race) who had won their freedom. Twenty-three million people had waited patiently for hours and in some places even for days to cast the first vote of their life, an affirmation of their dignity, citizenship and hope. Till then the majority of the people had been aliens in their own land. The elections were significant for the whole world: no liberation struggle had evoked so much passion and gained so much international support. The bombs of a white extremist group, which killed and maimed people on the eve of the elections, did not deter the people from the polls. The voting was orderly, which was highly significant when seen against the background of political violence in many parts of the country. Those who came from abroad to monitor the elections saw diverse peoples making a new nation of one people, wrote Ninan Koshy.[6]

These April 1994 days turned out to be more than just election days: the new South Africa was born in spirit as well as constitutionally. Apartheid had also brutalized the whites as it tried to destroy self-esteem of the blacks, robbing them of their humanity. Now humanity was on the way to being restored. This had shown itself in a multitude of ways: in the moving sight of an old black woman being propelled in a wheelchair and in a young black woman who threw her arms spontaneously around a young white woman as she emerged from the polling station and kissed her on the cheek. Elsewhere in the democratic world, elections are considered dull and a repetition of the already known. In South Africa, it was new, vivid, and real. It was an unforgettable experience.

The IEC performed an unprecedented task in organizing and supervising the elections. They had to prepare the elections in only four months, include millions of previously disenfranchised people, and work with a proper census of electoral roles. Also, negotiations with the Inkatha Freedom Party continued until the eve of the elections. There had been a great many uncertainties.

Several problems could perhaps have been foreseen. For instance, "defects" were built into the system and agreed to by all parties. The IEC was rightly preoccupied with political correctness, which was essential and strictly maintained. It was not matched by thorough logistical preparedness. This gave rise to irregularities in voting and in vote-counting. But this did not impair the fairness of the election and its results. The most striking aspect was how peaceful the elections were. As we stated in our report, "The success of the elections was primarily due to one reason, the determination of millions of people to cast their votes after centuries of struggle for their political rights. In the words of one voter: 'I have waited all my life for this day. No long queue is going to stop me.'"[7] On the basis of the many reports we received from the different EMPSA teams in the field, we could say,

There was a reverence about the voting and, for people of all faiths, there was a sense of God's gracious presence in history, healing, reconciling and giving hope for the future ... These elections have sent a message of hope for a new era in the history of South Africa; hope also for many other countries the world over, still struggling for justice and democracy.[8]

We did not feel that it was right for the churches to repeat what most other foreign observers had done by stating that the elections had been "free and fair"; we did not want to anticipate the final verdict of the IEC. So we decided to say that the elections had been an important step on the way to justice.

While peace monitors had been stationed throughout the country – along with observers from the UN, the Commonwealth, the EU, and the OAU – EMPSA's 65 teams of international monitors had already worked in key areas of political conflict, which had been intense since 1992, and thus they added a special dimension to the process. Sponsored by the churches in South Africa through the SACC, the South African Bishops' Conference and the Chapter of the World Conference on Religion and Peace, EMPSA was internationally supported mainly by the WCC. Our report stated,

It is because EMPSA has been with the people during the turbulent period of violence and the difficult stage of negotiations that it gained the confidence and respect of the communities. It is this confidence that made it possible for them to be of assistance at all stages of the electoral process. They took creative initiatives and intervened where necessary with sensitivity and care to enable and facilitate polling in many stations.[9]

Almost all churches in South Africa were used as polling stations. Indeed, the churches provided an extensive network throughout the whole of South Africa, which turned out to be of immense importance during the whole of the election period. Not only the church buildings but also the availability of so many pastors and priests and parish councils on whom we could count at all times meant that EMPSA was very privileged in its work. "EMPSA and the Eminent Persons' Group performed certain tasks in the election process which intergovernmental organizations were neither willing to do nor capable of performing."[10]

As members of the Ecumenical Eminent Persons' Group, we were particularly happy about the atmosphere in which we had worked, led by Kenneth Kaunda, former president of Zambia, and Joan Brown Campbell, general secretary of the National Council of the Churches of Christ in the USA. We had an excellent spirit of cooperation and felt strongly supported by the local churches throughout the election period. Beyers Naudé briefed us daily on the situation and inspired us with his insights.

Unfortunately, there was little time to make any fundamental recommendations to the WCC as the body that had sent us out. After my return, therefore, I wrote a personal letter to the general secretary of the WCC, Konrad Raiser, mentioning a few issues that seemed of importance for the attention of the WCC and its future support to the churches in South Africa and its first democratically elected government.

My feeling, based on discussions with church leaders and others in South Africa, was that the issue of the poorest of the poor needed immediate attention. The new government's first proposals and budget indicated a very cautious approach in order not to frighten away foreign investors. If the government were not going to deliver soon, the townships and the squatter camps, where the expectations were very high, could start a revolt, and the consequences for the government and the country as a whole could become disastrous. My suggestion was for the WCC together with the SACC and NGOs to enter immediately into negotiations on how the churches could be involved in government programmes and policies to help the poor on the basis of its basic document, *The Reconstruction and Development Programme*. The government needed all the support it could get from its allies in this first testing period, and an initiative by the WCC could be crucial. I also suggested that the Ecumenical Institute of Bossey should take an initiative by making a sizeable number of scholarships available to students from South Africa as a contribution to ecumenical thinking there.

I was strengthened in my opinion as it became clear already by the time of our departure from South Africa that the thinking of church leaders was developing along denominational lines, resulting in a weakening of the position of the SACC. Their earlier position of united resistance to the apartheid regime was already fading away. In addition, several church leaders, like Frank Chikane, SACC's general secretary, had been co-opted by the government to high positions and were thus no longer available to participate in discussions on the new responsibilities of the churches in their new-born nation. This had been a matter of real concern to all of us while we were together in EMPSA.

Raiser replied that he had had similar indications from his predecessor, Philip Potter, and that he hoped that we could soon meet to discuss these matters in more detail – a discussion that never, in the end, materialized.

13. The Truth and Reconciliation Commission: 1995-1998

"Scream as loud as you want; no one will hear you."[1]

The torturers in the apartheid jails were confident that knowledge of their crimes would never go beyond the cell walls. But the defeat of the apartheid regime opened up the opportunity for the victims to be heard.

The Truth and Reconciliation Commission (TRC) was created by the Promotion of National Unity and Reconciliation Act in 1995. It began its work in 1996 with 17 commissioners, a staff of 300, a budget of $18 million each year for two and a half years, and four large offices around the country. It was a political compromise and the result of hard bargaining between President de Klerk and the African National Congress (ANC) prior to the first democratic elections in 1994. Mandela had made it clear: "We can forgive, but we can never forget." The ANC wanted to avoid a trial of "war criminals" similar to the one at Nuremberg after the Second World War, which could have made those guilty of crimes into martyrs. De Klerk had eventually agreed with Mandela that there should be a commission that would grant individual amnesties on condition that the perpetrators revealed the truth and proved that their actions had been politically motivated. This compromise limited the powers of the TRC.

The TRC, working under enormous stress, operated through three interconnected committees: the human-rights violation committee, which was responsible for collecting statements from the victims and witnesses and recording the extent of gross human-rights violations; the amnesty committee, which processed and decided individual applications for amnesty; and the reparations and rehabilitation committee, which put forward recommendations for a programme of reparations.

Central to the process of restoring human dignity to relatives of victims and survivors was story-telling. The defeat of the apartheid system offered the opportunity for the suppressed anguish of the victims to be heard. "Now there is a chance for the whole world to hear the victims scream," observed Marlene Bosset of the Cape Town-based Trauma Centre for Victims of Violence and Torture.[2] And their screams would bring no fear of reprisal. Torturers were faced with the stories of their victims. The nation took responsibility for the suffering of the past. The TRC heard testimony from over 21,000 victims and witnesses, 2,000 of whom appeared in public hearings. The TRC also held special hearings of key institutions in society and their response to or participation in abusive practices. These hearings included the religious community and the armed forces. Four hours of sessions were broadcast live over national radio each day, and the "Truth Commission Report" television show on Sundays became the country's news programme with the greatest number of viewers.

Unfortunately, the TRC did not often use the strong powers it had at its disposal. It was sometimes accused of holding the mission of reconciliation above that of finding the truth. It was also strongly criticized for not issuing a subpoena against the home affairs minister and Inkatha Freedom Party president Mangosuthu Buthelezi, a decision largely based on the fear of a possible violent reaction. Despite these limitations, however, the hearings of the TRC were able to uncover a more detailed and credible picture of the torturers, murderers, and victims than any previous similar investigation any-where in the world. Over a period of more than two years, the com-mission revealed stories more horrific than most people had imagined.

With the appointment of Archbishop Tutu as chair and Rev. Alex Boraine (who briefly served on the PCR commission) as his deputy, the TRC acquired a semi-religious character. The notion of *ubuntu* (humanity; to live together; I am because you are) was writ-ten into the South African constitution. It was the guiding principle of the TRC: "A need for understanding but not for vengeance, a need for reparation but not for retaliation, a need for *ubuntu* but not for victimization."[3]

The work of the TRC rested on the view that reconciliation should be based on a public recognition of the truth. The honour of the vic-tims needed to be restored. Forgiveness could only take place if it was clear what had to be forgiven and if the perpetrator of the violence made a public confession. "In South Africa, forgiveness and remem-brance were supposed to go hand in hand: the acknowledgment of past atrocities would put the country on a sound moral basis and would lay the foundation for the building of a human-rights culture."[4]

The greatest innovation of the TRC, and the most controversial of its powers, was its ability to grant individual amnesty for politically motivated crimes between 1960 and April 1994. Yet many former per-petrators took the risk of not applying to the commission, particularly political leaders of the apartheid government and senior officers of the army. Those who declined to apply could still be prosecuted through the normal legal processes. The TRC tried to trace the responsibility to the top, and to persuade politicians to admit their mistakes.

The amnesty process was necessary. But how would past perpe-trators and their victims live together in a new society? This would require education; in particular it needed an understanding of how apartheid worked.

A major aspect of apartheid was that it focused not simply on black individuals but on entire black communities. But an important element was missing in the TRC's mandate: the forced removal of some 3.5 million Africans to the Bantustans. These people were not in a position to testify. Their communities had been forcibly shattered, dispossessed, and destroyed – all part of a systematic policy by the Pretoria regime. According to Mamdani,

> the TRC considered as a gross violation only that which was a gross violation under the laws of apartheid. ... Perhaps the greatest moral compromise the TRC made was to embrace the legal fetishism of apartheid. And to make little distinction between what is legal and what is legitimate, between law and right. And for post-apartheid South Africa, coming out of a history where crimes against humanity were upheld through a regime of law, it is vital and crucial to make this distinction.[5]

Amnesty was also seen in the light of the enormous socio-economic differences that still continue to exist in South Africa. The reconciliation promoted by the TRC was accompanied by a programme of socio-economic reconstruction, which was supposed to address the structural inequalities and consequences of apartheid – beyond the scope of the TRC. But it made only little progress. On the other hand, amnesty took immediate effect once it was granted. The relationship between victims and perpetrators thus remained unequal, which gave rise to criticism that reconciliation ultimately took place on the terms of the perpetrators and was devoid of justice. The reparations committee worked hard to put a programme in place, but it had only minimal funds available to match the enormous needs. This resulted in a great sense of frustration amongst the victims.

Also, there was a lack of cooperation on the part of two of the three main political constituencies – the (white) National Party and the Inkatha Freedom Party – which accused the commission of being biased in favour of the ANC. This had a negative impact on how the objective of the TRC – the promotion of national unity and reconciliation – was seen. In general, the white regime, both political and military, refused any collective responsibility for the gross human-rights violations that occurred, despite all the evidence given during the hearings.[6]

The TRC completed its work in 1998, with five volumes of careful analyses and findings. Mandela said, "We must regard the healing of the South African nation as a process, not an event..." The TRC, he said, "helped us to move away from the past to concentrate on the present and the future." And he added, "There is no question as far as I am concerned of a general amnesty, and I will resist that with every power that I have."[7]

Questions were raised as to whether forgiveness was a special characteristic of the African people or whether it was special to Mandela. Samora Machel's widow, Graca, who later married Mandela, believed that the people's attitude could have been very different without Mandela's leadership:

> He symbolizes a much broader forgiveness and understanding and reaching out. If he had come out of prison and sent a different message, I can tell you this country could be in flames. So his role is not to be underestimated too. He knew exactly the way he wanted to come out, but also the way he addressed the people from the beginning, sending the message of what he thought was the best way to save lives in this country, to bring reconciliation... Some people criticize that he went too far. There is no such thing as going too far if you are trying to save this country from this kind of tragedy.[8]

But Mandela's and Tutu's vision of forgiveness was not shared by all. For example, Charles Villa-Vicencio (national research director for the TRC who later created the Institute for Justice and Reconciliation) suggested,

> [I]t's too big a demand to make on anybody, to ask them to forgive – especially people who have suffered, who have been abused, or who have abused. That's a very deep, personal thing between people, and between people and God. I see reconciliation as much more modest: learning to live together and respect one another. That's the necessary groundwork, and I think it's all one can ask for. We have got to learn to be reconciled before we can forgive. We don't have to forgive in order to have peace... [and] political decency. But we've got to reconcile. Though I hope for much more,

this is enough. Still, the archbishop [Tutu] insists on forgiveness and perhaps the definition of reconciliation I use is an inadequate one. Perhaps it's going to take more.[9]

As another contemporary writer saw it:

Tutu has "Africanized" the concept [of reconciliation] in such a unique way that it shows up the usual Western Christian motive for reconciliation as sometimes being too far removed from the world to be of value. The Church says: "You must forgive, because God has forgiven you for killing His Son." Tutu says: "You can only be human in a humane society. If you live with hatred and revenge in your heart, you dehumanize not only yourself, but your community."

In the African *Weltanschaung* a person is not basically an independent solitary entity. A person is human precisely in being enveloped in the community of other human beings, in being caught up in the bundle of life. To be...is to participate.[10]

Truth and reconciliation commissions are not a replacement for prosecution, nor a second-best, weaker option when "real" justice is not possible. On the contrary, commissions can, and probably increasingly will, contribute positively to justice and condemnation of persecutions. Rather than a replacement for judicial action, therefore, truth commissions have often served as a complement to a weak judicial system, helping to fill the void created by the inaction, incompetence, or inability of the courts to even begin to handle the thousands of crimes that demand prosecution.[11]

For me, the importance of the TRC is that it placed some kind of truth on record. But many cases were not dealt with, and in others, key witnesses were dead. Worst of all, the political and military leaders responsible for the whole evil system evaded accountability. It is a scandal that the white military commanders and leaders of government, as well as big fish like Craig Williamson and Wouter Basson, were left unharmed, and today live as if nothing happened.

But in spite of all these shortcomings, the TRC was able to reveal enough to establish the essentials of the apartheid regime's crimes – the systematic torturing of prisoners, the state-sponsored death squads, dirty tricks, official lies and cover-ups, and the systematic corruption of the justice system. It has revealed enough to put South Africa's historical record straight so that future generations can be taught a history which is based on facts.

According to Allister Sparks, toward the end of the TRC hearings, a minister of the Dutch Reformed Church asked Archbishop Tutu to preach in his church. It was a significant invitation. The Dutch Reformed Church, the main denomination of the Afrikaner community, was a pillar of support for the apartheid regime: "the National Party at prayer." Moreover, the pastor was a chaplain in the defence force and thus an integral part of the regime's repressive machinery, while Tutu was a symbol of enmity to Afrikaners. Now the two were together before a congregation of Afrikaner notables. After the pastor spoke of the role of the Afrikaners in the past – stating that, despite mistakes, there was much to be proud of – Tutu in his sermon spoke of the "evil deeds" of the past and the need for a leader to step forward and help people to come to terms with what they had done. The pastor unexpectedly stepped forward: "I am not scheduled to speak now and actually I am not sure what I am going to say," he began. Then, turning to Tutu, he said, "As a minister of the Dutch Reformed Church for twenty years, as a chaplain in the defence force, I want to say to you we are sorry. For what we have done wrong we ask the Lord for forgiveness." He ended in a whisper, choked by tears. Tutu got up, put his arm around the distraught minister, and for an emotion-charged moment the two men stood there hugging each other as the congregation rose to its feet and applauded.[12]

The healing of the nation had begun.

14. In Retrospect

"Whether or not an action is right can only be
decided in loyal response to the call and guidance
of God in the present situation."
– *J.H. Oldham*

"We never can be anything more than a sign –
very limited, very humble – of the love of God."
– *Suzanne de Diétrich*

Reflections on a turbulent period

I have had the privilege of living unharmed through most of the crazy
20th century, with its two world wars and countless other conflicts.
The experiences I have had – and especially the ecumenical experience
to which I was exposed – transformed me and made me aware of the
lives of other people far less privileged than myself. I learned to resist:
against fate, dictatorship, violence, and racial discrimination. Resistance instead of resignation, in an attempt to protect our integrity.

Already as a boy of 13, when the Germans occupied my native country, I began to see the need to resist as we witnessed what evil people can do systematically to destroy the other. Very early on my family had to show their true colours and stand up for their convictions. It was then that the Christian faith became important to me and gave me spiritual strength. How did one live with an enemy? The enemy was first Nazism, of course, but later for me became apartheid and racism. The issue was how to resist these inhuman forms of life, which stemmed from intolerance, lack of respect for the other, and exploitation. The Jews and the gypsies were the scapegoats of the Nazis, as they had been the scapegoats for Germany's crisis in the 1930s and 1940s.

Since the war, we have been confronted with successive waves of global rebellions and third-world revolutions against Europe's ingrained belief in itself as the centre of civilization. Consequently, there was the need to decolonize and stop plundering the "third world"; to understand that our future depended on the well-being of *the world as a whole*. For the first time in history, we saw an increasingly integrated and universal world economy largely operating across state frontiers and frontiers of ideology. The globe was the primary operational unit, and there was tension between globalization and the inability of public institutions and the collective behaviour of human beings to come to terms with it.

Many of those who became involved in the ecumenical movement and the creation of the WCC had resisted Nazism during the Second World War. They had been engaged in hard and sometimes hopeless tasks. But they took risks. Some were committed Christians; others – like myself – only became Christians out of their involvement in resistance. Resistance became the only way of life against the deadly power of a Nazism that meant war, destruction, racism and genocide. Resistance was a way of survival. The Bible became an important means of nurture and helped in the resistance. But the end of the war did not mean the end of resistance.

In our situation of extremes, institutionalized racism and discrimination became an even greater obstacle to the unity of humankind. What we needed was not token integration, which is usually on the terms of the dominant culture, but the two-way process of receiving and giving to create a new relationship between people. For white people this meant that they had to be willing to pay a significant price. And it is here that the element of power came in. The white churches of the West knew about the sin of racism. Some, as a result of the PCR, did address the issue of power by looking at their investment portfolio and bank relations, others supported the WCC Special Fund to Combat Racism or analyzed church educational material on racism. This relation of racism to power was at the centre of PCR's programme. It meant a radical departure from the traditional concern for race relations, which in the past had concentrated more on personal relations between the races.

The struggle against racism has long been seen as a personal issue, and even today many people perceive it as such. One of PCR's aims has been to underline the fact that racism is also cemented into organizations and institutions, and that even church structures are not immune to it. We cannot speak of the unity of the Christian church and the oneness of the body of Christ if we continue to accept that we are divided on the basis of race, colour, and ethnicity. Therefore, the struggle against racism is not only a struggle *against* injustice and inhumanity; it is also a struggle *for* the integrity of the gospel and of the church of Jesus Christ. At that moment, racism becomes an ecclesiological issue because the integrity of Christian faith and praxis is at stake.

Almost 45 years after it was launched, there is clearly a need to evaluate and assess what the WCC has achieved through the PCR. I am aware that my role in doing so is limited, because as a former director of the programme I was too close to "the action": I was a *parti pris*. I am not and cannot be an independent observer of what happened.

The coming into being of the PCR was the result of a new awareness of the need to change racist structures and work for a redistribution of power. Post-colonialism and the emergence of the third world as a political and economic force demanded structural and institutional changes from the powerful West. White racism had its origins in the colonial period. Now that the colonies had become independent nations politically, new relations had to be forged. However, during the post-colonial period, racism persisted through more sophisticated economic and socio-political policies. We should not forget that the apartheid system was legalized after the Second World War in 1948, after the decolonization process had begun.

The concern over racism was on the agenda of the ecumenical movement from its earliest days. Historic gatherings at Jerusalem (1928), Oxford (1937), Evanston (1954), Cottesloe (1960), New Delhi (1961), Mindolo (1964), Geneva (1966), Uppsala (1968), Notting Hill (1969), and finally the 1969 Canterbury central committee – all these meetings took place in the socio-economic and political context of their time. The PCR was the result of much reflection at these different historical stations on the ecumenical journey. It signified a new departure and a new action model.

The racially oppressed as a yardstick

What has the PCR meant to the oppressed? This is the final yardstick according to which its work should be judged. I believe that the WCC, through the PCR, has given hope to the racially oppressed in many parts of the world: the black people of Southern Africa, Aboriginals in Australia, the Indians in Latin and North America, and Dalits in India. The churches and governments of the countries concerned have confirmed this. Specifically, it was the reason for the visit in 1990 of Nelson Mandela to the WCC in Geneva, during which he addressed the whole staff and expressed his special gratitude for the solidarity shown by the council toward the people of South Africa during the most difficult years of their struggle for freedom.

The PCR had to act boldly. We were to confess our faith through action – the mouth and the voice of the oppressed in the face of the powers that be. Our mandate was not to be afraid.

At the same time, it would be presumptuous to claim that the PCR succeeded in its task: all it could do was to indicate the direction in which the churches should go by providing an example. Churches taking a radical stand was exactly what racially oppressed groups expected after the initiative the WCC had taken. The sheer number of representatives of those groups who came to meet with the PCR in Geneva was stunning. Of course, they wanted to become the beneficiaries of the funds they knew were available. But there was more to it than that. Many of these groups had suffered from colonial policies – of their governments, of missions, and of missionaries. Most of them knew nothing about the WCC as an organization and were anxious to find out why and how it was breaking with the churches' past as they knew it. Could we in the PCR be trusted, or were we wolves in sheep's clothing? This was why PCR staff felt it was essential for these delegations to meet with other WCC colleagues to get a broader picture of the *raison d'être* of the council. In many respects the PCR became the eye-opener for all kinds of movements that had no tie whatsoever with the churches.

What was new was that the WCC gave the example to its member churches by creating a Special Fund to Combat Racism (partly from its own reserves) and by severing its relations with banks making loans to apartheid. It also radically cleaned up its investment portfolio.

In guiding the churches, we primarily addressed them as social institutions with substantial investments in the maintenance of the *status quo*. We pleaded for a serious consideration of economic disengagement from racist institutions. Through the PCR, the WCC provided an example for its member churches. At the same time, the soul-searching questions it needed to raise in relation to white racism had to be addressed to individual Christians and their institutions in the West – those that could influence their governments, banks, and multinational corporations.

We were part of a movement of resistance, trying to achieve more justice. And we knew well that in order to achieve that goal we would have to overcome much resistance from within the churches hampered by theological traditions and historical prejudices – and this would take more than one generation. Our task was not to change the world, but to help set up signs of hope along the road in the perspective of the kingdom. More was not possible.

The '60s to the '70s: A radical change in the political climate

This was a turbulent period of the WCC's history, and in retrospect we had to consider whether the member churches fully understood what they had asked the WCC to do by requesting it to take responsibility for a Programme to Combat Racism on their behalf. Equally important is whether the churches were ready to take their own responsibility to combat racism "at home." It was one thing to make strong statements: it was quite another to act and implement those words, and to combat racism on your own doorstep.

There were probably different reasons for the lukewarm response of some of the major churches involved, especially in Western Europe. One was, I believe, that most churches did not sufficiently understand what the aftermath of colonialism demanded of them in terms of radical change. In the 1960s our societies were in a revolutionary mood and many churches tried to understand and interpret that mood. They listened to the demands for change – change in the direction of a more just and participatory society, which had become one of the major themes of reflection in the WCC. The 1966 WCC world conference on Church and Society largely reflected the world's agenda and in many ways was preparatory for what the Uppsala assembly in 1968 was to decide. The Programme to Combat Racism, the Commission on the Churches' Participation in Development, and the Cooperation between Women and Men in Church and Society, Urban-Industrial Mission, Christian Education, and the Christian Medical Commission were all the result of that new understanding of responsibility in society. More than before, we were involved in contextual situations. We had seized on a moment of grace and opportunity (*kairos*), the favourable time in which God issues a challenge to decisive action.

The emphasis was on "people's participation" and "conscientization" and a church with and of (instead of for) the poor: the floor was theirs. The PCR was an expression of the ecumenical climate of that given period in history.

Because of the PCR's emphasis on action, the cooperation with local ecumenical groups was much stronger than with church hierarchies, whose influence declined. The increasing number of local networks and the possibility of communicating directly with these groups without having to pass through church headquarters was a new phenomenon. It contributed considerably to direct access to local situations and to hearing "the voice of (church) people." This is how much of the successful local fund-raising for the PCR could take place without the specific approval of church leadership, which was thus put under pressure. In fact, it meant a decrease in power of the central church structures, specifically in the West German situation.

Apartheid and communism

But in 1968 we also optimistically believed that we were well on the way to the Promised Land! Seven years later, at the 1975 WCC Nairobi assembly, we were, as our general secretary Philip Potter reminded us, "back in the desert." The political mood had dramatically changed. Liberation theologies were made to look suspicious and leftist – a dirty word. Politically speaking, WCC/PCR policies in support of the liberation of the peoples of Southern Africa were countered by fear among important sectors of many of the churches of the West. Was the WCC supporting Marxist movements in disguise, or at least movements influenced by Marxist ideology and trained and armed by the USSR and China? The Cold War between the communist East and the capitalist West deeply influenced political and church thinking. Fear became a major political element. Also, Western churches were concerned that political change in the Southern African region might destabilize NATO policies for protecting the strategic Cape route, which was part of its anti-communist strategy. Western church leaders were not immune to government pressure. What appeared to be "selective indignation" was a highly sensitive question within the WCC. At the time, it was hardly raised directly in the context of PCR policy decisions, and in other sectors of the WCC it had to be discussed in such a way as to avoid irritating the Eastern European churches and, in particular, the Orthodox.

The overwhelming optimism that preceded and followed the Uppsala assembly also brought major changes in the plans of many Western churches, and indeed in some churches in Eastern Europe. New programmes were created on racism, poverty, and human rights that were often linked into strong networks through the WCC. The growing Cold-War tensions, fueled by the Vietnam War and the nuclear-weapons stand-off on European soil, added to deep divisions on what the life and mission of the churches there should be. So, while delegates left the 1968 Uppsala assembly in a mood to work for a bold new mission in society, those leaving Nairobi in 1975 came home to the "desert," figuratively armed for battle!

In fact, PCR policy decisions were not at the centre of tensions at the Nairobi assembly: human rights in Eastern Europe were. The tone had been set by the results of a 1974 WCC consultation on human rights and Christian responsibility held in St Pölten, Austria, which dealt with the repression of Christians in Eastern Europe, especially in the USSR. And in the aftermath of Nairobi, the PCR became an essential element in keeping ecumenical dialogue across the Iron Curtain alive. Governments in Eastern Europe (often for the wrong reasons) found the participation of their nations' churches in the WCC unavoidable, in no small part because of the bold stance of the PCR, which they interpreted as anti-capitalistic and anti-Western. This helped to open doors for the WCC to engage in dialogue with government officials of religious affairs in Eastern Europe, which at times contributed to reducing church-state tensions and fostering international ecumenical dialogue. The Eastern European churches' participation in the WCC was of course conditional on the approval of their respective governments.

Some would say that the PCR created conflict within the churches as well as between the churches and the WCC by bringing into the open issues such as redistribution of power, violence and non-violence, just rebellion and just war. These areas were usually avoided because they were too sensitive for discussion; the existing social and economic order was not to be disturbed. Churches were fearful of explicitly touching on the economic and political realm lest they create disunity in the congregations and thus spoil the fellowship. One could even add that churches were afraid of losing funds. However, I believe it would be better to say that the PCR put already existing differences of opinion onto the table, thus stimulating an important learning process. Churches had to learn to live with different attitudes to ethical questions among their members. More than that: they had an obligation to help formulate ethical issues as well as give possible answers. Otherwise, they condemned themselves to tacitly supporting the *status quo*.

One particularly interesting feature of PCR was the participation of secular and ecumenical groups, including Roman Catholic orders and dioceses, in conscientization and fund-raising projects. This was especially the case in West Germany and the Netherlands. Some secular groups had lost all hope in the church: in their eyes, the churches had always been part of the "establishment," often siding with the oppressors.

The PCR opened up the discussion on violence and whether there is such a thing as "just war" and "just rebellion." Churches had to make judgments and distinguish between the violence of aggression and oppression, and the right to self-defence. The choices confronting the churches were not between violence and non-violence, but between justice and injustice, because there can be no peace without justice. The alternative to violence is not non-violence, but justice.

The discussion about how economic links with South Africa strengthened the apartheid regime sparked off a much broader discussion on the responsibility of churches and Christians in economic life. The involvement of multinational corporations in South Africa was only one criterion for judging an investment portfolio. Other criteria were involvement in the production of armaments, the social policy of a company, and its policies in the third world. Not only corporations and banks but the whole economic system came under biblical judgment. This discussion, which started with the issue of economic links with South Africa, eventually led the WCC to set up the Ecumenical Development Cooperative Society: EDCS granted loans to economically viable projects, mainly in the developing countries, which met a set of social criteria. Through the EDCS model, the WCC tried to show how the margins of the economic system can be used to combine financial return with high social return.

I am convinced that many victims of racism looked with respect and appreciation on the work of the PCR. But at the same time they saw these actions only as a small beginning, too little and too late. They asked more: justice, not cheap reconciliation; cultural identity, not cultural domination; parity, not charity; trade, not aid; economic reciprocity, not social generosity; economic independence, not dependence. Churches still have a long way to go to achieve credible Christian witness in the world today. Confessing our faith is more than finding the right words and formulations. It means challenging injustice and getting angry, taking sides and taking risks, creating visible signs of solidarity. That is what racially oppressed people expected from us.

Some leaders of the liberation movements, as we have seen earlier, had been educated largely in mission schools. They were in the best sense of the word the "products" of the mission. Oliver (OR) Tambo, acting president of the ANC during Nelson Mandela's imprisonment, told me he felt very strongly that PCR was contributing to what the gospel was about: the *liberation of people*. How I would have liked to hear that kind of statement from the mouth of a church leader! And one of our problems was precisely how to convey this message to the churches: how to help them transform their conception of what they often called "terrorist" organizations into liberation movements?

In fact, this became one of the most difficult parts of our "mission": to try and make churches and missions understand that, by proclaiming the gospel worldwide, they were contributing in an effective way to a movement among the oppressed to free themselves from the bonds of oppression, and no longer politely accept hand-outs. The churches needed to recognize and be proud of this liberation process for which they themselves were partly responsible. Did they really understand the deep biblical meaning of "liberation"? That this was not something limited to individuals but equally valid for whole peoples? This is what liberation theology is about.

Desmond Tutu reminded us,

> We are involved in the black liberation struggle because we are also deeply concerned for white liberation. *The white man will never be free until the black man is wholly free*, because the white man invests enormous resources to try to gain a fragile security and peace, resources that should have been used more creatively elsewhere. The white man must suffer too because he is bedevilled by anxiety and fear and God wants to set him free, to be free *from* all that dehumanizes us together, to set us free for our service of one another in a more just and open society in South Africa.[1]

One of the principal reasons for racism is its relation to power, domination, and class. In South Africa, apartheid as an ideology was based on reducing people to "black," "coloured," or "Indian," and as such making them inferior beings. They were people who could therefore be dealt with under an endless number of laws and rules. Any right to decide about their own lives was taken away from them. Thus they could be parked in the Bantustans or used in the mines under the most inhuman conditions, without any rights. "Inferior" non-white people depended completely on the whims of the "superior" white people who decided on their future. Apartheid was a system of institutional racism, exploitation, and cheap labour. It was contrary to the gospel and needed to be abolished. As the oppressed people became more and more aware of their situation, they organized themselves and started to resist. At that point the churches should have recognized more clearly their right to resist and shown their understanding and solidarity, which unfortunately was not the case.

I must confess that I had not anticipated so much resistance to real change on the part of the churches and so little understanding for what was at stake. There was an enormous defence mechanism at work. And even if there was understanding, there was also a continuous fear of public opinion: "How are we going to defend taking a radical stand? How will this affect our image as churches?" Though the PCR provided considerable written material and its staff did what it could to inform the WCC's constituency, there was a lack of communication between the WCC and its member churches and, even more, between church leadership and local congregations. If we explained clearly enough, and even better if we were able to have the victims speak out themselves at the local church level, there was understanding and solidarity. Local ecumenical and anti-apartheid groups often became the spearhead and the initiators for action; they put church leadership under pressure. Grassroots organizations became the backbone of our efforts.

Unresolved questions

Today, we wear the 20th century rather lightly. We memorialize everywhere: exhibits, inscriptions, theme parks on the past. But these are either nostalgic or triumphalist, praising famous people or recollecting selective suffering. The message is that all this is now behind us and that we may now advance unencumbered by past errors into a different and better era. This does not help our appreciation and awareness of the past: it becomes a surrogate. We need to give the present a meaning by reference to the past. We look back upon the 20th century as an age of tragic political mistakes and wrong choices. But are we not mistaken? We have the illusion that we live in a time without precedent: that what is happening now is new and that the past has nothing to teach us.[2]

There seems to be a general fear in our society: of the foreigner, the outsider, the black, Islam, mass immigration, terrorists, change, open frontiers, free exchange of ideas. And that fear is used by political parties and governments to their own advantage. This is territory ripe for racism, and for finding a scapegoat. There is also the danger that we think we have learned enough from the past to know that many of the old answers don't work. This may be true. But the past helps us understand the perennial complexity of the questions we are trying to deal with today. If we can no longer find adequate solutions to our problems because they are too complex, we still have to discover how to live through our times with our unresolved problems.

White racism is a particular problem of the West. Most churches in the West have lived in and been part of a capitalist society. During my time, the PCR was what it was because it focused on one particular issue: white racism, particularly in South and Southern Africa. (I should add that in this book I have only been able to deal with South Africa: ideally, more attention should have been given to the liberation of Southern Africa, i.e. Angola, Mozambique, Namibia, and Zimbabwe.)

With the release of Mandela in 1990 and the first democratic elections in South Africa in 1994, the political situation there changed dramatically. But what has really changed for the black people of South Africa in everyday life? Apartheid was legally abolished by one of the world's most progressive constitutions. Parliament and government changed from a white to a black majority. Impressive social improvements were made, like running water and electricity for millions of people living in the townships. But the transition from liberation politics to democratic politics, from freedom fighters to citizens of a democracy, has been difficult. The liberation movement, in order to facilitate the struggle, had at the time to oversimplify socio-economic and political problems as white-black issues. Ambiguity could not be tolerated. But once a democracy came into being, conflicts of interest and tensions between different groups in society needed to be addressed. The principle of equality within the democracy was often undermined by a sense of entitlement to govern after years of oppression. Loyalty to the historic liberation movement in the face of large-scale corruption by the new leadership who claim to be on the side of the poor, and evidence of breaking the law, have proved major obstacles and created increasing cynicism among the poor. The gap between poor and rich did not disappear; rather it increased with a new class of rich blacks joining the already existing rich whites. New divisions came into being. The benefits of the new order are only very slowly reaching those who need them, and understandably this slowness causes enormous frustration and anger among millions of people.

Barney Pityana, a former director of PCR, believes that democracy itself is in danger. He quotes Hannah Arendt, who describes the situation of "total domination" by one party as the precursor to a totalitarian state.[3]

So once again, what has changed in South Africa? Apartheid has legally gone. Democracy has been put in place. But poverty has remained and increased. And so has the divide between rich and poor. The "trickle-down effect" has not taken place. As the SACC triennial conference in February 2014 stated,

> We are deeply concerned about the ever increasing corruption, service delivery protests and unrest and violence it is bringing upon our land. Particularly disheartening is the fact that innocent people are dying at the hands of those who are supposed to care for them ... [W]e express our deep concern over the widening gap between rich and poor in South Africa. We are therefore not surprised by the strikes and protests emerging from the mines and other sectors of business and society. Inequalities in society are bound to lead to social instability and this is what we are seeing daily in our country.[4]

In retrospect, the WCC felt that it had done its duty by helping to empower a black democratically elected government. South Africa had become a constitutional democracy. But can we say that racism has been overcome when the neo-liberal ideology in the particular situation of South Africa has stayed in place? We ignored the much wider issue of the neo-liberal global market, which often uses race as a front. The churches, through the WCC, the World Alliance of Reformed Churches (now the World Communion of Reformed Churches), and other world or regional bodies have faced this issue, and different WCC consultations have criticized neo-liberal globalization. However, the latter were speaking to the WCC and not on behalf of it.

The WCC's 1998 assembly in Harare clearly linked globalization to colonialism and included a critique of neo-liberalism as a competing vision to the *oikoumene*. It also included an affirmation of the God of life integrating the ecological dimension and social justice.

Similar strong statements were made by the World Alliance of Reformed Churches in Accra in 2004 and the WCC's 2013 assembly in Busan.

The PCR has never condemned any economic system *a priori*. The analytical approach by PCR has been rather to point out in an *inductive* manner what economic institutions have been involved in supporting racism. At the 1969 Notting Hill consultation on racism, one participant said,

> We do not speak here of the need to reform, for a gentle rearranging of systems and practices. Rather we are raising questions concerning the very premises on which the society is based – questions on the nature of capitalism, for example. Does the free enterprise system in fact depend upon the existence of a scapegoat class, currently the black man?[5]

Racism does not flourish only in capitalist countries; it exists in all societies. But apartheid in South Africa was probably one of the most extreme examples of the capitalist system. Given the WCC's constituency, there would have been little room for taking up in-depth the sensitive issue of neo-liberalism as such at any point. In fact it might have killed the whole PCR by giving critics the excuse of labeling it a socialist undertaking. We had to act responsibly. But at the same time, we must remember that the issues of power and capitalism will have to remain on the agenda of the ecumenical movement if we are serious in overcoming racism.

We believed that in South Africa the African National Congress, once it had won the elections, would, as part of a government of national unity, introduce the necessary reforms and thereby limit the excesses of the existing capitalist economy. However, it did not and probably could not, given the fact that after the fall of the Berlin wall and the defeat of communism and the USSR in 1989 there was no alternative left to the new South African government but to accept the already existing neo-liberal and free-market system that it inherited from the apartheid period.

We would be mistaken in believing that the present situation of gross inequalities in South Africa can continue without widespread outbreaks of violence, such as those following the Marikana killings in 2012. Equally, the question of unjust land distribution will have to be addressed. The South African churches, the SACC, and other partners in South African society, such as the trade unions, are waking up to the situation and will at one point or another have to draw the necessary conclusions.

Kairos Southern Africa, in a statement of 27 April 2014 entitled "What hope is there for South Africa after twenty years of freedom?", states,

> Certainly this is a moment to once again say another big thank you to brothers and sisters across the world who sacrificed so much so that South Africa's people may be free. As South Africans, we ask that this solidarity now be passed on to the people of Palestine so that they may also be free. In South Africa, we were convinced that the freedom of white and black people [is] inextricably linked … and today we are again convinced that the freedom of the people of Palestine and Israel are also inextricably linked … As Christians and people of faith, we have to answer the question: What [is it] about our national life, what about our country, [that] gives us hope? Is there any reason to hope? This is not a question about optimism, but about a deep and abiding hope … There are signs that the church is slowly reawakening to its prophetic role in society … We have to stop impunity, corruption and mismanagement in [their] tracks before we can go the way of other countries … South Africans, who gave birth to our dynamic democracy and who still dream about a non-racial and non-sexist society, have been very vocal when things have gone wrong in our democracy, and this too is a sign of hope. This should not stop but should increase and

intensify until we build the South Africa that Madiba (Mandela) would have been proud of.[6]

This statement is indeed an encouraging indication of the continued concern and involvement of Christians in South African, who now extend their solidarity to the people of Palestine and elsewhere. We will never forget what the people of South Africa have taught the *oikoumene* about resistance and solidarity.

The WCC decided to concentrate on white racism, with particular emphasis on Southern Africa. But that did not mean that white racism was not an issue elsewhere. It is prevalent in many other parts of the world, though, as we have seen, the reasons for singling out Southern Africa during the past period were obvious. It must be said that the PCR also gave considerable attention to white racism in Europe in a later period, which I have not described because that period came after my time.

The role of the WCC: past and present

During the 1960s, 1970s, and 1980s, the WCC was listened to. The voice of the WCC counted, especially when sensitive and politically hot issues like poverty, peace, disarmament, liberation, gender, racism, and apartheid were raised. Public opinion reacted – sometimes vehemently – through the media. But the WCC mattered. It had received a mandate from the churches to take worldwide initiatives, thereby challenging the churches themselves. The mandate of the WCC, recognizing the importance of the role of the laity in the council, also foresaw lay advisers, invited for their competence on specific matters, for example at central committee and other commission meetings. Often better equipped to deal with socio-economic and political issues, they assisted the WCC in formulating policies and programmes. Their insights were crucial for taking policy decisions.[7]

The WCC had a pioneering role. The second half of the 20th century saw the revolutionary and some would say the prophetic years of the ecumenical movement: the aftermath of the war, post-colonialism, and the Vietnam War. The launching of the PCR in 1969-70 was no doubt one of the strongest examples of the mandate that the churches had given the WCC.

Today, the situation has completely changed. After 65 years of existence, the WCC has lost its pioneering role; its original mandate has changed. It has become a bureaucracy. It no longer takes initiatives on its own: it now depends on its member churches for that. And its decision-making process has been modified from a system of majority vote to one of consensus-building. In practice this means that the council no longer has a cluster of supporting churches around an initiative for a specific programme or project. The situation is more diffuse. Burning issues about which there is no unanimity, like gender, can often not be discussed in any depth. We can add to this today's much more complicated and dangerous world economic and political situation, which would probably have rendered difficult an initiative like the PCR in the 1970s. Perhaps the PCR has even contributed to the changes that have taken place in the WCC as described above.

Churches, in turn, have lost much of their influence in society, at least in the West, and realistically speaking it looks likely that the WCC will not regain its earlier influence. We cannot expect things from the council that it can no longer deliver.

But other forms and expressions of ecumenism do exist and may take its place. There could be a plurality of groups, and a new division of responsibilities divided among different organizations instead of a concentration in one organization, as has previously been the case.

One thing looks certain: far from the time when we thought we were on the way to the Promised Land, we seem still to be wandering in the desert, nervously looking for the next oasis. Present world economic and political crises and the rise of populism, nationalism, ethnicism, and protectionism have added to insecurity and fear, presenting an unprecedented challenge to the *oikoumene*. The ecumenical movement no doubt needs new ways of expressing itself. However, the burning issues from the past and especially the present – like water, climate change, ecology, and new forms of energy – remain unchanged. They bang relentlessly at our doors and will not go away: they need to be answered.

As to the PCR as a means of combating racism, it has served its purpose. One important result has been that dozens of local, national, and regional ecumenical racial justice initiatives have come into being and have developed their own policies and programmes. They meet together and keep each other informed through networking. The WCC performs a coordinating role, and this is exactly what needs to happen.

My personal involvement in the PCR

For me personally, all this and much more was over the years translated by what *oikoumene* is about: the search for the unity of humankind. I felt an enormous sense of responsibility and at the same time a personal fulfilment, in spite of all the uncomfortable questions we had to raise around racism and the negative reactions we received. I can only express my special gratitude for the fellowship and support I experienced in the ecumenical movement, even though relations necessarily went through deep points of crisis and uncertainties. Our understanding of what needed to be done was not always unanimously agreed upon. We had to search for new ways of acting and accept that sometimes there were different ways of reaching the same objective of racial justice.

I learned a hard lesson: if you speak out for something you believe in, you have to be willing to pay a personal price of not being understood, of losing the support of friends. It was not always easy to be philosophical about those who expressed contempt for the PCR and me personally. I had to learn not to take myself too seriously. It was an exciting but also a turbulent time. But by meeting and listening to the victims of racism, they gave me new energy to bear witness to injustice. We had to amplify the voices of the victims and develop respect for their cultures and customs. South Africa was under my skin – and it remains so. It was a place I could not leave behind. It was a nightmare; there were feelings of guilt over white Western history and also much anger. Putting uncomfortable questions to the churches in the West was sometimes understood as disloyalty to your own church and also to your own family and origin, and at times this was painful.

The task was formidable. I could contribute to new ideas, and my adrenaline went up! I received many invitations to speak to congregations, students, synods, and local ecumenical and anti-apartheid groups. We needed a mix of firmness and diplomacy, though the latter was not always our strongest point! And I must admit that several times I felt like giving it all up. It was too much, it was too complicated, and there were too many sensitivities around; too much politicking. But there could be no question of surrendering. We had to go on resisting. Without the support of my wife and close family, I would not have been able to continue for long. There was a great deal of strain that we had to share among ourselves as staff. I look back to my time at the PCR with deep affection for my colleagues, whose support and sense of team spirit were imperative.

Daring faith

M. M. Thomas, in his moderator's report to the Nairobi assembly in 1975, said,

> Let us not forget that our struggle is not merely against others but also against ourselves, not against flesh and blood, but against the false spiritualities of the idolatry of race, nation, and class, and of the self-righteousness of ideals which reinforce collective structures of inhumanity and oppression.[8]

This reflection has preoccupied me more and more since my work in the PCR. We easily see the evil of racism elsewhere but forget how much we are part of the problem ourselves. None of us are exempt from thinking in terms of "we" and "they," the "in" and the "out" group. Fear of change, open borders and the unknown, Islam and terrorism – these are issues our populist politicians use shrewdly when they praise security and nationalism and demand a stop to what they call "massive immigration." The fear of no longer being amongst ourselves. Populism and nationalism do indeed feed collective structures of oppression.

We should not forget that South Africa was *pars pro toto*. The task is far from finished. As world crises intensify, so will expressions of fear and hatred, discrimination and racism.

As we continue to combat racism, we are not only faced with the neo-liberal market thinking and overkill of information, but also with the corruption of the very political class that pretends to defend the poor. Statements by governments, trade unions, multinationals, and even churches, including ecumenical bodies, sound hollow and are no longer taken seriously. There is a general lack of credibility that unfortunately leads to much indifference and cynicism in the Western world.

In the face of this, it seems imperative for the future that we do not give up what we engaged in over the years. By nature we are not prone to resist: we prefer consensus. Our society educates us to obedience. But there comes a moment when we can no longer consent or compromise. We have to say no: no to the destruction of life, to injustice, to the misuse of power. We have learned from history that resistance is a way of life. We may have to find new forms of resistance as we engage in hard and sometimes hopeless tasks. Resistance has to continue as long as there is a threat to humanity, violence against human life. To resist is in the first instance to keep alive the fragile flame of life. It is not necessarily something heroic or secret, an underground movement. It can be the most natural reflex for pure self-protection. But what matters most when we are faithful to the gospel is the liberation of people and the defence of values, without which there is no life possible. The responsibility of human beings for each other extends to the whole of humanity throughout time.

There is an inseparable connection between confession and resistance. Dietrich Bonhoeffer discovered this in the early 1930s in Nazi

Germany and decided that in that situation there was a further step to be taken. For Christians, he said, resistance ultimately means:

> not just to bandage the victims under the wheel, but to put a spoke into the wheel itself. Such action would be a direct political action, and it is only possible and desirable when the church sees the state fail in its function of creating law and order, i.e. when it sees the state unrestrainedly bring about too much or too little law and order.[9]

His statement strongly influenced the declaring of the *status confessionis* by the churches in the struggle against apartheid. It also strongly influenced me and my colleagues working in the WCC, trying to translate into action the connection between confession and resistance. This was at the heart of the decision by the WCC when it launched its Programme to Combat Racism.

Notes

Chapter 3: Geneva, 1958-1981

1. W. A. Visser 't Hooft, *No Other Name: The Choice between Syncretism and Christian Universalism* (London: SCM Press, 1963), 95.

2. Ibid., 113.

3. Thanks to the initiative of "l'éminence grise," Pastor Marc Boegner, president of Cimade, and Visser 't Hooft, a secret plan was drawn up called Operation Angola, involving a small and well-selected number of committed Cimade team members, which made it possible for these students to leave Lisbon illegally in 1961 and cross Salazar's frontiers into Franco's Spain using real/false Senegalese passports. See Charles Harper, "L'Afrique lusophone et la Cimade en 1961: l'engagement de la Cimade dans les luttes d'indépendances des colonies portugaises," Paper delivered during the study day organized by CIMADE in Marseilles, 4 June 2010.

4. *In a Strange Land, a Report of a World Conference on Problems of International Migration and the Responsibility of the Churches, Leysin, Switzerland, 11-16 June 1961* (Geneva, WCC, 1961).

5. It is hardly believable that as I was focusing on the issue of migrant workers and the local congregation, the WCC was simultaneously conducting a study on "The Church for Others," about which I knew nothing. The migration secretariat would have benefited enormously from the insights of that study, and, in turn, our practical experience might have been a useful contribution. Communication within the WCC left something to be desired.

6. Heyde and I became close friends. He later joined the Churches' Committee on Migration in Western Europe on behalf of the EKD and made a substantial contribution to the committee's work. He died unexpectedly in 1969.

7. The Conference of European Churches (CEC) was hesitant to get involved in social and economic issues and was not yet ready to take on such responsibility. See, *Within Thy Gates, report of the conference on migrant workers in Western Europe, Arnoldshain, Western Germany, 10-15 June 1963*, (Geneva, WCC, 1964).

Chapter 4: Uppsala, 1968

1. Michael Kinnamon and Brian E. Cope (eds), *The Ecumenical Movement: An Anthology of Key Texts and Voices* (Geneva, WCC Publications, 1997), 294.

2. Ibid., 296.

3. James Baldwin, "White Racism or World Community," in *The Uppsala Report 1968*, ed., Norman Goodall (Geneva: WCC, 1968), 130.

4. Ibid., 65.

5. *Uppsala 68 Report* (Geneva: WCC Publications, 1968), 270.

Chapter 5: Notting Hill and Canterbury, 1969

1. See Robert N. Faris, "A Changing Paradigm of Mission in the Protestant Churches of Mozambique: A Case Study of Eduardo Mondlane" (PhD thesis, University of Cape Town, 2007).

2. Declaration of Revolution by George Black and other black power representatives. Report on the WCC-sponsored consultation on racism, Notting Hill, London, 19-24 May 1969, to the WCC Central Committee, August 1969.

3. *Minutes of the WCC Executive and Central Committees, Canterbury, August 1969* (Geneva: WCC, 1969), 271-77.

4. Resolutions on intergroup relations, in *The Evanston Report: The Second Assembly of the WCC 1954* (London: SCM Press, 1955), 158-60.

Chapter 6: From Consultation to Confrontation: The 1970s

1. Letter from E. C. Blake to members of the WCC executive committee, 3 November 1969.

2. Theodore Gill, "Clarence Jones: 'I have a dream' of justice through nonviolence," WCC Press Centre, 27 August 2013.

3. David Gill (ed), *Gathered for Life: Official Report of the Sixth Assembly of the World Council of Churches* (Geneva: WCC, 1983), 206.

4. Elisabeth Adler, *A Small Beginning: An Assessment of the First Five Years of the Programme to Combat Racism* (Geneva: WCC, 1974).

Chapter 7: Priorities and Staff Relations: 1970-1981

1. C. F. Beyers Naudé, "The Parting of the Ways," *Pro Veritate*, 15 October 1970.

2. *Minutes of the Central Committee, Canterbury, August 1969* (Geneva: WCC, 1969), 273.

3. *Minutes of the Central Committee at Addis Abeba* (Geneva: WCC, 1971), 55.

4. Ibid., 246.

5. Albert Luthuli attended the International Missionary Conference at Tambaram in 1938 and was elected chair of the Natal Missionary Conference in 1941, before he joined the ANC in 1944.

6. Alan Paton Centre and Struggle Archives: PC 1/10/1/2—"In Memoriam Albert Luthuli," the funeral speech by Alan Paton.

7. *The Christian Mission in Relation to Industrial Problems*, Vol. 5 of the The Jerusalem Meeting of the International Council (New York: IMC, 1928), 144.

8. J. Merle Davis (ed), *The Economic Basis of the Church*, IMC Tambaram Report (London: Oxford UP, 1939), 600.

9. Ibid.

10. *The World Council of Churches and Bank Loans to Apartheid* (Geneva, WCC-PCR, 1977), 32-33.

11. "WCC Ends Relations with Three South Africa Related Banks," WCC Press Release, 8 September 1981.

12. In the context of the WCC seeking alternatives for banks that supported the South African regime with loans, it is interesting to note that this discussion contributed in an important way to the creation of the Ecumenical Development Cooperative Society, later renamed Oikocredit.

13. *Ecumenical Involvement in Southern Africa: A Survey of Responses by Member Churches to Resolutions by the WCC Central Committee on Investments, White Migration and Bankloans* (Geneva: Cetim, 1975).

14. Walter Rodney, *How Europe Underdeveloped Africa* (London, Bogle-L'Ouverture Publications, 1972).

15. Frantz Fanon, *The Wretched of the Earth*, transl. Constance Farrington (New York: Grove Press, 1963).

16. *The World Council of Churches and Bank Loans to Apartheid* (Geneva: WCC-PCR, 1977).

17. Alexander Kirby, *South Africa's Bantustans: What Independence for the Transkei?* (Geneva, WCC-PCR, 1976).

18. Martin Luther distinguished between two kingdoms: the worldly kingdom of the state that governs through rules and regulations in society, and the spiritual kingdom that abides with God's reconciliation between the world and humankind through the gospel's liberating force.

19. *Financial Mail*, 21 October 1977. Quoted in "South Africa's Hope – What Price Now?" Background paper (Geneva: WCC-PCR, December 1977).

20. "South Africa's Hope – What Price Now?" Background paper (Geneva: WCC-PCR, December 1977).

21. Ibid., 1-2.

22. "Statement commended by the central committee of the WCC, August 1973," *The Ecumenical Review* 25:4 (October 1973).

23. I am particularly grateful to my German colleague Konrad Raiser, then director of Unit II on Justice and Service (of which the PCR was one of the sub-units), who took the main responsibility in trying to appease the relations between the WCC and the EKD during that whole period.

24. Philip A. Potter, "Report of the General Secretary," in Gill, *Gathered for Life*, 208.

25. *Christians in the Technical and Social Revolutions of Our Time: World Conference on Church and Society: Official Report, Geneva, 12-26 July 1966* (Geneva: WCC, 1967), 115.

26. David Gill, "Violence and non-violence," in *Dictionary of the Ecumenical Movement*, 2nd ed. (Geneva: WCC Publications, 2002), 1192.

27. M. M. Thomas, *My Ecumenical Journey 1947-1975* (Trivandrum: Ecumenical Publishing Centre Private Ltd., 1990), 412.

28. J. Panagopoulos, *Prophetic Vocation in the New Testament and Today* (Leiden: E. J. Brill, 1977), 226-27.

29. Paulo Freire, *Pedagogy of the Oppressed* (New York: Herder & Herder, 1970, and New York: Seabury Press, 1970). Transl. from *Pedagogia do Oprimido*, 1968.

Chapter 8: Support and Criticism

1. Erica Meijers, *Blanke Broeders-zwarte vreemden* (White Brothers – Black Strangers: Netherlands Reformed Church, Reformed Churches in the Netherland and the Apartheid in South Africa 1948-72), (Hilversum: Uitgeverij Verloren, 2008).

2. *Racism in Theology and Theology against Racism, 1975 WCC Report of a Consultation on Racism* (Geneva: WCC, 1975).

3. Colleen Ryan, *Beyers Naudé: Pilgrimage of Faith* (Grand Rapids, IL: Eerdmans, 1990), 144.

4. Pauline Webb, *World Wide Webb: Journeys in Faith and Hope* (Norwich, UK: Canterbury Press, 2006), 110-11.

5. Letter to J.A. Hebly, 30 November 1974.

6. *Amsterdam to Nairobi: The World Council of Churches and the Third World* (Washington, DC: Georgetown University Ethics and Public Policy Center, 1979).

7. Leon Howell, "A Profile in Consistency," *Christianity and Crisis*, 2 March 1981, 36.

8. Ibid.

9. Ibid., 38.

10. John Bennett, "Neoconservative 'Realism' vs. Third-World Realities," *Christianity and Crisis*, 12 November 1979.

11. Paul Abrecht, "Church and Society Replies to its Critics," *The Christian Century*, 27 February 1980.

12. "Statement on Land Rights," Doc. 2.4, WCC Central Committee, Geneva, 1982.

13. "Land Is Our Life," WCC-PCR Consultation, 7-13 May 1989, pp. 5, 12.

14. J. Briggs, M. A. Oduyoye, and G. Tsetsis (eds), *A History of the Ecumenical Movement: Vol. 3, 1968-2000* (Geneva: WCC, 2004), 362-63.

15. Gill, *Gathered for Life*, 152-53.

Chapter 9: At the ILO: 1982-1987

1. Craig Williamson was given an unexpected amnesty in 2000 after appearing before the Truth and Reconciliation Commission (TRC). He was charged with the murders of two women academics, Ruth First (the wife of Joe Slovo, who was one of the leaders of the South African Communist Party and who became a cabinet minister in the first government after the 1994 elections) and Jeanette Schoon, as well as Schoon's six-year old daughter Katryn. In addition, it was well known that Williamson was involved in several bomb attacks, mainly against ANC offices in Africa and Europe. Williamson was seen as not having told the truth to the TRC and outrage was expressed by many apartheid victims after the announcement of the verdict.

2. ILO Staff Regulations: Chapter I, Duties, obligations and privileges, art.1.2, January 2014.

3. Baldwin Sjollema, *Isolating Apartheid. Western Collaboration with South Africa: Policy Decisions by the World Council of Churches and Church Responses* (Geneva: WCC-PCR, 1982).

4. Francis Blanchard, *L'Organisation international du travail: de la guerre froide à un nouvel ordre mondial* (Paris : Editions Seuil, 2004).

Chapter 10: The Kairos Document: 1985

1. *The Kairos Theologians* (Braamfontein, South Africa, September 1985).

2. Theo Witvliet, *Het Kairos-Document en de moderne Theologie- een nabeschouwing* (The Hague: Baarn, 1988).

3. Theo Witvliet, *Het Uur van de Waarheid: Het "Kairos-Document" van Zuidafrikaanse christenen* (The Hague: Baarn, 1986).

4. *The Kairos Document – Challenge to the Church: A Theological Comment on the Political Crisis in South Africa* (Kairos Theologians, Braamfontein, 1985), 17.

5. Ibid., 19.

6. Ibid., 23-24.

7. Ibid., 28.

Chapter 11: The End of Apartheid Rule: The 1990s

1. See related interview: "Desmond Tutu: A God of Surprises," from *On Being: With Krista Tippett*, http://www.onbeing.org/program/desmond-tutu-a-god-of-surprises/transcript/6185.

2. C.F. Beyers Naudé: "The Role of the Church in a Changing South Africa," in *The Road to Rustenburg: The Church Looking Forward to a New South Africa* (Cape Town: Struik Christian Books, 1991), 227.

3. Michael Kinnamon (ed), *Signs of the Spirit, Official Report of the Seventh Assembly of the WCC* (Geneva: WCC, 1991), 219.

4. *Report of the Ecumenical Eminent Persons Group to the World Council of Churches/South African Council of Churches*, 4 May 1994.

Chapter 12: Elections in South Africa: 1994

1. *The Guardian*, 3 May 1994.

2. In Allister Sparks, *Tomorrow is Another Country: The Inside Story of South Africa's Road to Change* (Chicago: University of Chicago Press, 1996), 7-8, 12.

3. *The Guardian*, 3 May 1994.

4. Ibid.

5. Ibid.

6. "Electoral Triumph: South African Vote Out Apartheid," *One World*, July 1994, p. 4.

7. *Report of the Ecumenical Eminent Persons Group to the World Council of Churches/South African Council of Churches*, 4 May 1994, 3.

8. Ibid., 2, 4

9. Ibid., 4.

10. "Electoral Triumph," *One World*, 5.

Chapter 13: The Truth and Reconciliation Commission: 1995-1998

1. Charles Villa-Vicencio, paper on "The Truth and Reconciliation: Its Theological Challenge," quoting Marlene Bosset, 5.

2. Ibid., 5-6.

3. Anthony Sampson, *Mandela: The Authorized Biography* (London: Harper-Collins, 1999), 529.

4. Michelle Parlevliet, "Background of the Truth and Reconciliation Commission," in *Truth and Reconciliation in South Africa and the Netherlands*, Special Issue 23 of SIM (Utrecht, 1999), 64.

5. See Mahmood Mamdani, *The TRC and Justice, Truth and Reconciliation in South Africa and the Netherlands*, Special Issue 23 of SIM (Utrecht, 1999), 37.

6. Parlevliet, "Background," 76-77.

7. Sampson, *Mandela*, 532.

8. Ibid., 533.

9. Nathan Schneider, "More than Politics, Interview with Charles Villa-Vicencio," *The Immanent Frame*, 19 November 2010. http://blogs.ssrc.org/tif/2010/11/19/more-than-politics-charles-villa-vicencio/.

10. Antjie Krog, *Country of My Skull: Guilt, Sorrow, and the Limits of Forgiveness in the New South Africa* (New York: Broadway Books, 2000 [1998]), 110.

11. Priscilla B. Hayner, *Unspeakable Truths: Facing the Challenge of Truth Commissions* (New York: Routledge, 2002).

12. Allister Sparks, *Beyond the Miracle: Inside the New South Africa* (London: Profile Books, 2003), 169.

Chapter 14: In Retrospect

1. Cited by John W. de Gruchy, *Bonhoeffer and South Africa* (Grand Rapids, MI: Eerdmans, 1984), 74.

2. Tony Judt, *Reappraisals: Reflections on the Forgotten Twentieth Century* (London: Penguin, 2008), 5-20.

3. Barney Pityana, "Vote 'No' to the Nightmare of Zuma's ANC, " *Mail and Guardian*, 2 May 2014.

4. South African Council of Churches Triennial Conference Statement, 25-26 February 2014.

5. Barbara Rogers, *Race: No Peace without Justice* (Geneva: WCC/PCR, 1980), 105-106.

6. Kairos Southern Africa statement, 27 April 2014.

7. I think of the role of economists like Jan Tinbergen, Jan Pronk, and Harry de Lange, but equally of people such as Pauline Webb, Elisabeth Adler, Marga Bührig, Margaret Mead, Justice Annie Jiagge, Eduardo Mondlane, Z. K. Matthews, Bola Ige, M. M. Thomas, André Philip, Max Kohnstamm, and Jacques Ellul, to mention only a few.

8. M. M. Thomas, "Report of the Moderator," in *Breaking Barriers, Official Report of the Fifth Assembly of the WCC, Nairobi, 1975* (London/Grand Rapids, MI: SPCK/Eerdmans, 1976), 240.

9. Quoted by Konrad Raiser, "Bonhoeffer and the Ecumenical Movement", in de Gruchy, *Bonhoeffer for a New Day,* 319-39.

Index

UNITA, National Union for the Total Independence of Angola, 80, 82, 97
United Nations, 28-29, 90-91, 94, 95
United States, 6-7, 9, 21, 39, 41, 97, 137-38
Unity, Christian, 24
Utrecht, 3, 4, 8, 10, 15, 27

Van den Heuvel, Albert, 24, 61
Van der Veen, Rein-Jan, 69, 116, 118
Van der Zee, Wim, 161, 165
Van Es, Wim, 35
Van Hoogstraten, Jan, 4, 8
Vatican Council, Second, 24, 39
Verghese, Paul, 58, 70
Vienna, 16-19
Viljoen, General Constant, 156, 165
Villa-Vicenzio, Charles, 160, 179
Vischer, Lukas, 24, 104, 127
Visser 't Hooft, W. A., 22, 23, 24, 25, 26-28, 39, 40, 45, 52, 58, 61, 63, 64, 89, 109, 119
Von Wartemberg, Bärbel, 106
Von Weiszäcker, Richard, 89
Vorster, John, 75,124
Vose, Bill, 138

Waldensian church, 34, 35
WCC Assemblies. See Assemblies
Webb, Pauline, 58, 59, 65, 66-67, 74, 118
Weber, Hans-Ruedi, 106
Williamson, Craig, 124,131, 180, 207
Witte, Bartold, 161
Woods, Archbishop Frank, 59
Worker priests, 33-34
World Alliance of Reformed Churches, 101, 113, 195-96
World Council of Churches
  assemblies. See Assemblies
  central committee 26, 57-59, 65, 66, 70-71, 76-77, 104, 126
  criticism of, 119-25, 150
  executive committee, 57-59, 74, 82, 88, 89, 104-107
  Geneva, 10, 20-21
  and race, 44, 111

World Federation of Trade Unions, 138
World Student Christian Movement, 93
World War II, 2-3, 11, 69, 72, 183
World YWCA, 140

Young, Andrew, 60, 68, 70

Zimbabwe, 39, 47, 69, 70, 79, 83, 97, 107, 122, 136, 194